To

———————————————————————

From

———————————————————————

21 IRREFUTABLE PRINCIPLES OF PURPOSE

21 IRREFUTABLE PRINCIPLES OF PURPOSE

FEMI OYEWOPO

ACHIEVERS WORLD

21 Irrefutable Principles of Purpose

Copyright © 2018 by Femi Oyewopo.

All rights reserved.

Requests for information should be addressed to:
femi@femioyewopo.com

This book, or parts thereof, may not be reproduced, stored in a retrieval system, or transmitted in any form or by any means, electronic, mechanical, photocopying, recording or otherwise, without the written permission of the publisher.

ISBN 978-0-6482834-0-9 (paperback)
ISBN 978-0-6482834-3-0 (hardcover)
ISBN 978-0-6482834-1-6 (ebook)
ISBN 978-0-6482834-2-3 (audiobook)

Printed in Australia

Acknowledgments:

Every attempt has been made to credit the sources of copyrighted material used in this book. If any such acknowledgment has been inadvertently omitted or miscredited, receipt of such information would be appreciated

Unless otherwise indicated, all Scripture quotations are taken from the Holy Bible New King James Version, © 1979, 1980, 1982, 1984 by Thomas Nelson, Inc. Used by permission. All rights reserved.
Scripture quotations marked (CEB) are taken from the *Common English Bible*. Copyright © 2011 by Common English Bible. Scripture quotations marked (CEV) are taken from *Holy Bible: Contemporary English Version*. Copyright © 1995 American Bible Society. Scripture quotations marked (ESV) are taken from the *Holy Bible, English Standard Version*, copyright © 2001 by Crossway Bibles, a division of Good News Publishers. Used by permission. All rights reserved. Scripture quotations marked (GNT) are taken from the *Holy Bible, Good News Translation*. Copyright © 1992 by American Bible Society. Scripture quotations marked (ISV) are taken from the *Holy Bible, International Standard Version*. Copyright © 1995–2014 by ISV Foundation. All rights reserved internationally. Used by permission of Davidson Press, LLC. Scripture quotations marked (KJV) are taken from the *King James*

Version of the Bible. Scripture quotations marked (MSG) are taken from *The Message*. Copyright © 1993, 1994, 1995, 1996, 2000, 2001, 2002 by Eugene H. Peterson. Scripture quotations marked (NAS) are taken from the *New American Standard Bible*, copyright © 1960, 1962, 1963, 1968, 1971, 1972, 1973, 1975, 1977, 1995 by the Lockman Foundation. Used by permission. Scripture quotations marked (NCV) are taken from *The Holy Bible, New Century Version*. Copyright © 2005 by Thomas Nelson, Inc. Scripture quotations marked (NIrV) are taken from *New International Reader's Version*. Copyright © 1995, 1996, 1998, 2014 by Biblica, Inc.® Used by permission. All rights reserved worldwide. Scripture quotations marked (NIV) are taken from *The Holy Bible, New International Version*. Copyright © 1973, 1978, 1984, 2011 by Biblica, Inc.® Used by permission of Zondervan. All rights reserved worldwide. www.Zondervan.com. Scripture quotations marked (NKJV) are taken from *The Holy Bible, New King James Version*. Copyright © 1982 by Thomas Nelson, Inc. Scripture quotations marked (NLT) are from the *Holy Bible, New Living Translation*. Copyright © 1996, 2004, 2007 by Tyndale House Foundation. Used by permission of Tyndale House Publishers Inc., Carol Stream, Illinois 60188. All rights reserved. Scripture quotations marked (NRSV) are taken from the *New Revised Standard Version Bible*. Copyright © 1989 by the Division of Christian Education of the National Council of the Churches of Christ in the United States of America. Used by permission. All rights reserved. Scripture quotations marked (RSV) are taken from the *Revised Standard Version of the Bible*. Copyright © 1946, 1952, 1971 by Division of Christian Education of the National Council of Churches of Christ in the United States of America. Used by permission. Scripture quotations marked (TLB) are taken from *The Living Bible*. Copyright © 1971 by Tyndale House Publishers, Wheaton, Illinois 60188. All rights reserved.

Words and phrases in Scripture quotations that are in **bold** or *italics* are the emphasis of the author.

DOWNLOAD THE TOOLBOX FREE

Just to say thanks for buying my book, I would like to give you the Ultimate Self Discovery Toolbox version 100% FREE!

TO DOWNLOAD GO TO:

http://femioyewopo.com/21ipop_toolbox

GREAT QUOTES ABOUT PURPOSE

"There is a great identity crisis among students today. Who am I? What is the purpose of life? Where did I come from? Where am I going? The Bible has a direct answer to this great big philosophical question and unless God seals the vacuum among youth today, then some other ideology will, because young people must have a faith. They must believe in something to find fulfillment in their lives."
~Billy Graham, Billy Graham

"We are all different. Like the sun, the moon, and the stars, God has created us to be different from one another, and He has done it on purpose. Each of us meets a need, and we are all part of God's overall plan."
~Joyce Meyer

People who use time wisely spend it on activities that advance their overall purpose in life.
~John C. Maxwell

The value of life is not in its duration, but in its donation. You are not important because of how long you live, you are important because of how effective you live.
~Myles Munroe

"God made you as you are on purpose. He gave you your looks, your height, your skin color, your nose, your personality. Nothing about you is by accident. … God calls you His masterpiece."
~ Joel Osteen

DEDICATION

This book is dedicated first and foremost to God. I praise Him for "making me so wonderfully complex."

The book has been more than 20 years in the making. I am full of gratitude that God has finally helped me to make it happen.

I am grateful to God for my kind hearted, loving and highly supportive wife, Oludotun Adesola Omolewa, and my lovely kids, King David and Father Abraham. We have been on this journey of purpose together and this could not have been a reality without your help and your committed support. Thank you also for believing in me.

I am grateful to God for my parents who have been there from the beginning, my siblings and their families for your encouragement.

I am grateful to God for hundreds of teachers and mentors whom he had used, and still using, to SHAPE my life and to help me learn the truth contained in this book.

I am also grateful to God for YOU!

Before you were born, God planned this moment in your life. It is not by accident that you have come in contact with this book at this very moment in your life.

With God, accidents are not accidental and coincidences are not coincidental.

God wants you to discover His grand plan and purpose for your life... both now and in eternity.

My earnest desire, prayer and expectation are that the book will be a blessing to your life.

CONTENTS

Copyright |

Acknowledgments |

Free Toolbox Download |

Dedication |

Principle #1: There Is A Purposeful Creator | 19

Principle #2: Every Person Has A Purpose | 23

Principle #3: Purpose Precedes Creation | 31

Principle #4: You Don't Decide Your Purpose | 37

Principle #5: Discover Your Purpose By Revelation | 41

Principle #6: Not Every Purpose Is Known | 55

Principle #7: When Purpose Is Not Known... | 63

Principle #8: Every Purpose Has Its Time…| 69

Principle #9: Purpose Determines Potential | 75

Principle #10: Purpose Determines Provision | 81

Principle #11: Purpose Is Inbuilt and Inherent | 85

Principle #12: Your Purpose Is Necessary | 91

Principle #13: Purpose Is General and Specific | 99

Principle #14: No Purpose Is Better ….| 105

Principle #15: Purpose Is Source of Fulfillment | 111

Principle #16: Purpose Is Often Multiple | 115

Principle #17: Purpose Is Interdependent | 121

Principle #18: Purpose Is Permanent | 125

Principle #19: Purpose Is a Preservative | 131

Principle #20: Purpose Determines Demand | 137

Principle #21: Purpose Determines Reward | 145

APPENDIX 1

APPENDIX 2

APPENDIX 3

INTRODUCTION

WHAT IS YOUR PURPOSE?

In the context of this material, your purpose is the original intention or reason in the mind of God for creating you. Your purpose is your life assignment and your life calling.

The above statement presupposes that you are not an accident or a product of chance, blind nature, evolution or a "big bang". Your purpose was pre-determined, your life was planned, and your creation was meticulously designed and accomplished.

Irrespective of what you feel about yourself or anyone feels about you, you are unique, special, and original.

There are two most important days in your life: The day you were born and the day you discovered WHY you were born. Also, there are five most important questions of life that bother everyone. No one can have a meaningful and fulfilling life without answering ALL of these five questions.

This book will help you discover definitive answers to these questions and move on from just existing to really living.

INTRODUCTION

Each of the 21 Principles of Purpose that are provided in this book is a piece of the puzzle that has eluded mankind from generation to generation. For the first time, in a single volume of book, the principles are being handed over to you.

When you read this book and embrace each of the principles, the puzzle of life will unravel right before you and your life will never be the same from that point forward. The unraveling of the puzzle is the beginning of a new life adventure for you.

The understanding of these principles will help you to find the clarity, the wisdom and the courage to be who you are created to be and to do what you are created to do.

I used to be a shy, super introvert with a very low self-esteem until I discovered these principles. I then found out that that there is an inexhaustible deposit of possibilities that God had hidden in me waiting to be explored, developed and deployed. The resources that God has placed in you for your generation are absolutely inexhaustible. It is time to take a big plunge to discover and explore!

I welcome you to a new and exciting life of meanings and adventures.

To Your Success

Femi Oyewopo

PRINCIPLE #1
THERE IS A PURPOSEFUL CREATOR

You were made by God and for God, and until you understand that, life will never make sense.
- Rick Warren, bestselling author of
The Purpose Driven Life book

THERE IS TIME AND THERE IS ETERNITY.

Time is a chunk of measurable period carved out from endless eternity. Time can be measured but eternity cannot. Time has a beginning and an end but eternity does not. Time can be divided into three segments: past, present, and future. The past is in the tomb but the future is in the womb – today is all we have.

In the beginning God created the heavens and the earth **(Genesis 1:1).**

In the timeline of time, a point was designated as "the beginning." The preceding scripture verse answers one of the fundamental questions of life: "From where did we originate? " It is a question about source or origin.

The verse also shows that "the heavens and earth" have not always existed. A specific time called "the beginning" was given as the point when the heavens and the earth came into existence by the creative act of God.

The Source of all Creation

Genesis 1:1 fundamentally and eternally settles the question of the source of creation –God!

In the beginning was the Word, and the Word was with God, and the Word was God. He was with God in the beginning. Through him all things were made; without him nothing was made that has been made **(John 1:1-3, NIV).**

This scripture verse builds on the foundation of Genesis 1:1. It states that ALL things were made by the word of God and that NOTHING was made without Him.

The phrase "all things" is very bold and absolute because the word "all" means ALL. God is the Creator of ALL things. Absolutely everything in the universe has its source in God. Not a single thing or being came into existence without Him.

He Created both Visible and Invisible World

Everything was created by him, everything in heaven and on earth, everything seen and unseen, including all forces and powers, and all rulers and authorities. All things were created by God's Son, and everything was made for him.. God's Son was before all else, and by him everything is held together. **(Colossians 1:16-17, CEV).**

Notice that this passage is more specific by stating that God created the visible and the invisible world. He created both visible beings and invisible beings like angels. It also stated that God is the ultimate source of all life, powers, and authorities that are demonstrated by any being at any level in the entire universe
(Psalm 75:6, Romans 13:1, Daniel 4).

Before I made you in your mother's womb, I knew you. Before you were born, I chose you for a special work. I chose you to be a prophet to the nations. **(Jeremiah 1:5, ERV).**

One of the best ways to understand this verse is to look at our physical world and study how building construction or manufacturing is done. Production usually starts in the research and development department. They are supposed to research and discover the need in the market. The product development team will then design the product before the production team takes the design and turn it into a real product through the manufacturing process. This explanation seems over simplified but it is meant to paint the picture of the basic processes involved in the manufacturing of a product. Product manufacturing usually follows a general guideline of need discovery, product design and testing, and then production.

He Decides the End before the Beginning

God says in **Jeremiah 1:5**, *"Before I formed you in the womb I knew all about you."*

You made all the delicate, inner parts of my body and knit me together in my mother's womb. Thank you for making me so wonderfully complex! Your workmanship is marvellous—how well I know it. You watched me as I was being formed in utter seclusion, as I was woven together in the dark of the womb. You saw me before I was born. Every day of my life was recorded in your book. Every moment was laid out before a single day had passed - **(Psalm 139:13-16, NLT).**

According to the above verse, all the days of your life were already prewritten in God's book before you drew your first breath. The scriptures paint a very vivid picture of an extremely detailed and meticulous Creator who does careful planning before forming a person in the womb. He even has books where He writes and draws before He creates. That is why He says in **Isaiah 46:10:** *"From the beginning I revealed the end. From long ago I told you things that had not yet happened, saying, "My plan will stand, and I'll do everything I intended to do"* **(GW).**

In other words, He finishes the design before He starts the creation. God is the Creator of ALL things, and He is a purposeful Creator.

PRINCIPLE #2
EVERYONE HAS A PURPOSE IN THIS WORLD

"The greatest tragedy in life is not death, but a life without a purpose." **- Dr Myles Munroes**

Before I made you in your mother's womb, I knew you. Before you were born, I chose you for a special work. I chose you to be a prophet to the nations - **(Jeremiah 1:5, ERV).**

God had a conversation with a young man called Jeremiah who later became a well-respected prophet in Israel. At the time of the conversation, this young man had no thoughts whatsoever about becoming a prophet. Then God came on the scene and told him that He created him and before He formed him in the womb He knew all about him. Moreover, His intention for creating him was to make him a prophet to the nations.

Before we take a careful look at the above scripture, it is necessary to first refer to a statement of Jesus Christ:

Later, Jesus spoke to the people again and said, "I am the light of the world. The man who follows me will never walk in the dark but will live his life in the light.- **(John 8:12, Phillips).**

I refer to this scripture because as human beings, we should understand that in respect to life, we are nice people who are working in the dark of the night. We cannot find our way without light. Jesus said He is the Light of Life or the light needed to find the way through the pathways of life.

Your word is a lamp to guide my feet and a light for my path. - **(Psalm 119:105).**

Jesus replied, "There are twelve hours of daylight every day. During the day people can walk safely. They can see because they have the light of this world. But at night there is danger of stumbling because they have no light- **(John 11:9-10, NLT).**

Light brings illumination. It represents knowledge, understanding, and the wisdom to make the right decisions and to follow the right pathway at every crossroad of life.

Light helps us to know what we are supposed to do and what we don't have any business getting involved in. Light also means the revelation or unveiling of what is hidden or unknown. It is difficult or even impossible to see our way in the darkness without light but when light comes everything becomes clear.

In a room that is totally void of light, you might be confused and disoriented. Perhaps, you may walk towards a wall thinking you are walking towards the door. Without light, there is a complete loss of direction. Can you imagine a situation where a pilot's navigation equipment suddenly packs up? He or she would end up in the middle of NOWHERE LAND!

The Five Most Fundamental Questions of Life

Light also represents THE TRUTH! We live in a world that has been overtaken by the darkness of lies and deception. However, the Word of God gives us reliable answers to the five most fundamental questions of life:

Who am I? – A question of IDENTITY

Where am I from? – A question of SOURCE or ORIGIN

Why am I here? – A question of PURPOSE

Where am I going? – A question of DESTINY

What can I do? – A question of POTENTIALS and CAPABILITIES

Your ONLY reliable source to find answers is the Word of God, which is the Light of Life!

Satan, who is the god of this world, has blinded the minds of those who don't believe. They are unable to see the glorious light of the Good News. They don't understand this message about the glory of Christ, who is the exact likeness of God **(2 Corinthians 4:4)**.

He (The Devil) was a murderer from the beginning. He has always HATED THE TRUTH, because there is NO TRUTH IN HIM. When HE

LIES, it is consistent with his character; for HE IS A LIAR and the father of lies - **(John 8:44b).**

There are many lies and deceptions in the world about the fundamental questions of life but the Word of God is the truth and the light for life. There is a proactive action by the Devil to always block you from the truth because ignorance and deception are the Devil's age-long tools for holding people in captivity.

Laying a solid foundation to establish the source of TRUTH and AUTHORITY in this chapter is very important. It helps us to build our understanding of the source and purpose of creation on the revelation truths from the Word of God, not on the lies of this world and the god of this world.

There are very important revelations or truths about the birth process and the purpose of human life that are brought to light in **Jeremiah I: 5**:

1. God formed you in your mother's womb.

2. Before God formed you; He knew all about you. He planned your creation with purpose and intention on His mind.

3. Before you were born, He appointed your assignment and sent you into this world to accomplish that assignment or purpose for which He created you.

4. Before you were born, He empowered you with all the gifts, talents, and potentials that you will ever need to fulfill your purpose and your assignment in this world.

EVERYONE HAS A PURPOSE

You might not feel that your life has any purpose or you might not know what your life purpose is. However, that does not change the eternal truth that your life is not a chance of nature. You are a creature of purpose. You were born because there is an assignment for you to fulfil. The fact that you are still alive is evidence that your assignment is yet to be completed.

Irrespective of the situation or circumstance that led to your conception, God formed you in your mother's womb for a purpose. He knew all about you even before you were conceived.

There are specific examples in the Bible where God gave parents the rare privilege of getting a glimpse of the purpose and assignment of their babies even before those babies were conceived or while they were still in the womb.

1. SAMSON (JUDGES 13.2-5)

Although Samson's parents were old and past the age of childbearing, the angel of God told them they would have a baby boy who would be a warrior and a leader. He would be God's agent to defend the Israelites from their enemies. This information was given to Samson's parents before his conception.

2. SOLOMON.

Before David had his son, Solomon, God told him that Solomon would build the temple in Jerusalem.

3. JOHN THE BAPTIST – (LUKE 1:13)

John the Baptist's parents were also old and past the age of childbearing. Yet, the angel of God appeared to Zacharias, John's father, and told him that his wife would have a baby boy.

He was given a preview into the assignment of the child: he would be the forerunner of the promised Messiah and he would demonstrate the spirit and power of Elijah.

Zacharias was also given a specific name for the child when he was born.

At birth, Zacharias' family suggested that the baby be called Zacharias after his father. However, Zacharias and his wife, Elizabeth, insisted that his name would be John according to God's instruction to them.

This is a great example of how people can actually have a wrong idea or opinion about what is supposed to be your life purpose.

4. JESUS CHRIST – (MATHEW 1: 21-25)

Before Jesus was conceived, Mary, who was a virgin and engaged to be married, was told that she would become pregnant without having sex with any man; she would have a baby boy. This baby boy was Jesus Christ – the promised Messiah.

Joseph, who was at that time engaged to Mary, received the same information. He became Jesus' "earthly father."

These are examples of people whose purposes and assignments were revealed by' God even before their mothers conceived them. All of these examples are meant to establish the fact that God is a purposeful Creator and that there is a purpose for every one born into this world.

In Galatians 1:15, Paul, testified to the fact that God called him from his mother's womb to be an apostle. Paul started his life not knowing his purpose and even worked against it. His entire life was transformed when he discovered that there was a purpose for him.

PRINCIPLE #3
PURPOSE PRECEDES CREATION

Before I made you in your mother's womb, I knew you. Before you were born, I chose you for a special work. I chose you to be a prophet to the nations - (Jeremiah 1:5, ERV).

GOD BEGINS WITH THE END IN MIND

Although the principle that purpose precedes creation was mentioned earlier in the book, we will discuss in further depth the meaning and implication of it.

Jeremiah 1:5 is a very important and foundational scripture to support this principle.

In this verse, the word "*before*" was mentioned twice:
1. "Before I formed you in the womb, I knew you"
2. "Before you were born, I set you apart and appointed you a prophet to the nations."

If we apply the concept of the manufacturing process that we looked at earlier to this scripture, once again, we will notice how crucial it is to define purpose before creation. The application of the eternal truth in this passage is that there is a purpose for your life. Your purpose was determined and clearly defined before you were formed in your mother's womb. Furthermore, you are designed for a purpose, and you are the best for your purpose.

You might feel that you don't have anything good or special to offer or that you don't have what it takes to be successful. You are not alone. Many people feel that way. We did not design or create ourselves so usually, we start out in life not knowing who we are and how much we are capable of doing. Often, we are ignorant of our gifting and potentials.

Jeremiah experienced the same thing in Jeremiah 1:5. He probably thought: "A prophet needs to be bold, vocal, and knowledgeable but I don't have any of these qualities. Moreover, most prophets I know are old people and I am just a young man."

God had to rebuke Jeremiah. He told him: "Don't say you are too young to handle the responsibility that I have given you. I created you, and I have fully equipped you for this role."

What we do naturally is that we compare ourselves to other people, and we focus on the talents that they have. Alternatively, we focus on the things they can do that we can't. Such attitudes can limit us from becoming the best we can be.

When God called Moses and gave him a role as God's agent of deliverance to the children of Israel from their Egyptian slave masters, Moses felt absolutely incapable and unqualified to do the job. God had to also tell him, "I created you; I know the capabilities I have put in you, and I have prepared you for this role."

In the book of **Judges Chapter 6**, an angel of the Lord appeared to a fearful young man who was hiding in the caves because he was afraid of the army of the Midianites.

When the angel of the Lord appeared to Gideon, he said, "The Lord is with you, MIGHTY WARRIOR."

"Pardon me, my lord," Gideon replied, "but if the Lord is with us, why has all this happened to us? Where are all his wonders that our ancestors told us about when they said, 'Did not the Lord bring us up out of Egypt?' But now the Lord has abandoned us and given us into the hand of Midian."

The Lord turned to him and said, "GO IN THE STRENGTH you have and save Israel out of Midian's hand. AM I NOT SENDING YOU?"

The angel that appeared to Gideon looked beyond his low self-esteem and called him by the name he was created to be. The angel said to him, "MIGHTY WARRIOR." Gideon obviously felt embarrassed and unqualified to be called such a name. He later discovered that the mighty warrior God created him to be was within him like a sleeping giant! That potential was waiting for the opportunity to express itself. Gideon's perspective about himself changed because he finally believed what the angel said about him. He later became a great leader who went into battle against thousands with just 300 soldiers and came out victorious.

Just like Gideon you may also feel fearful, timid, and even struggle with low –self-esteem. You may even feel that you don't have the skill, talent of the training to accomplish what God has created you to do. I want to reassure you that that feeling is not unique to you.

Most of the great people that we look up to and admire also started with fear and self-doubt. The only difference is that they acted on the conviction in their heart, despite the fear playing up in their head. That is what makes the difference for everyone.

I also started out as a very timid super introvert. I started out questioning my abilities to lead, speak and write books. But inside me is this conviction that *"You are created to be a published author. There are books in you that you need to write."*

As I began to follow my passion for reading, researching, collating, organizing and sharing information, I discovered that I have the gift to simplify and communicate the knowledge that I have acquired. I discovered that I have the ability to transform texts and information to diagrams, and pictures. Then opportunities, platforms and responsibilities began to lay demand on my teaching abilities. As I began to see the positive impact of my teaching gift on my listeners, my confidence began to develop. It is like a feedback mechanism. But it all started by taking action. It started by following my passion and deploying my potential.

Another secret that i discovered in this process is that the more I use my potential, the more it grows. The more my potential grows, the more results I see. And the more results I see, the more my confidence increases. It is like a chain reaction. But that chain reaction starts by stepping out to use what you have got, no matter how small it is. So start where you are with what you have.

I conclude this chapter with David's awesome statement:

Your eyes saw my unformed body: all the days ordained for me were written in your book before one of them came to be - **(Psalm 136: 16).**

PRINCIPLE #4
YOU DON'T DECIDE YOUR PURPOSE, YOU ONLY DISCOVER IT.

THE MANUFACTURER DECIDES

The world is filled with a large population of people who are living by trial and error. They are unhappy and busy trying to figure out what they should be doing with their lives. Understanding the principle in this chapter is the antidote to a boring or confused lifestyle that is void of happiness and fulfillment.

In Jeremiah 1: 5, God revealed the truth that only He could make the decisions about your purpose. It is also revealed that this decision is made before your formation in the womb.

This principle is in compliance with the creation, manufacturing, and even the building construction process. It ensures that the product is manufactured in compliance with a predetermined purpose and design. That is why it is very important for you to know you are not a creature of accident. Such knowledge is very reassuring; it will have a huge impact on your perspective about yourself and your self-esteem.

In Jeremiah 1: 6, Jeremiah tried to argue with God and to lecture Him about the fact that He had come for the wrong guy. Jeremiah felt that he did not have any of the attributes required to do what God was asking him to do.

Fast forward to Jeremiah 10: 23 to a mind blowing discovery that Jeremiah made about life:

(NOW) I know LORD that people's lives are not their own: it is not for them to direct (or decide) their (own) steps - **(Jeremiah 10: 23). (Emphasis in brackets and capital letters are mine)**

Understanding and affirming this verse will free you from worrying and trying to figure out the purpose of your life. Trying to determine your purpose is a responsibility that is far bigger than you. Your life is not your own. God created every living thing and gave life to all of them (Nehemiah 9:6). In Him we live, move and have our being (Acts 17:28). It is not within your power and your ability to decide what your life purpose is. God has already established that. All the days of your life were already decided before you were born (Psalms 139:6).

In Hebrew 2: 1-2, we are encouraged to have the mindset of Jesus as far as our lives on earth are concerned. How do we know what Jesus' mindset is? We can capture it by what He said and did. Jesus made the following statements about Himself:

1. I am sent

2. I have come to do your will according to what is written about me

3. Let your will be done, not my will

4. My desire is to do the will of Him that sent me and to FINISH HIS WORK.

As stated earlier, God has already decided your purpose before you were created, thus you don't decide it. You were designed, created and empowered for His purpose. That is why trying to do what you are not created for is like trying to put a round peg in a square hole. It's a misfit. Can you imagine how uneasy and unfulfilling such a life would be? Failure to understand purpose is the major reason people live boring and unfulfilled lives. Your responsibility is to discover what your purpose is and commit yourself to fulfilling it.

How do you know what is God's purpose for your life? You know your purpose by **discovering it**.

How do you discover your purpose? That leads us to the next chapter.

See you on the other side!

PRINCIPLE #5

PURPOSE IS DISCOVERED BY REVELATION

Now when Jesus went into the region of Caesarea Philippi, He asked His disciples, "Who do people say that the Son of Man is?"

And they answered, "Some say John the Baptist; others, Elijah; and still others, Jeremiah, or [just] one of the prophets."

He said to them, "But who do you say that I am?"

Simon Peter replied, "You are the Christ (the Messiah, the Anointed), the Son of the living God."

Then Jesus answered him, "Blessed [happy, spiritually secure, favoured by God] are you, Simon son of Jonah, because flesh and blood (mortal man) did not reveal this to you, but My Father who is in heaven **(Matthew 16: 13-17, AMP)**

THE MANUFACTURER KNOWS.

The word "revelation" means to unveil, to bring to light or to make known what is unknown.

In **Jeremiah 1: 5- 6**, we noticed that Jeremiah was unaware of what his life purpose was until God spoke to him about it. The fact remains that the purpose of a product is in the mind of the manufacturer of the product. What a manufacturer usually does is to make the information about a product available to other people through what is called the manufacturers manual.

David said in **Psalm 139:16, (NLT):**

You saw me before I was born. Every day of my life was recorded in your book. Every moment was laid out before a single day had passed.

In **Matthew 16:17**, Jesus asked His disciples "Who do people say I am?" Jesus' disciples told Him people said He was a prophet just like Isaiah, Jeremiah, and other prophets. Jesus went on to ask His disciples for their own opinions of Him. Peter responded by saying that Jesus is the Christ, the Son of the living God. In response, Jesus told Peter that flesh and blood (human being) did not reveal that truth to Him, only God in heaven.

The implication of this statement is that there are two basic sources of the knowledge we have:

1. Physical source through the physical sense organs

2. Spiritual source by revelation from God unto the human spirit

Proverbs 20:27 says, "*The spirit of man is the candle of the LORD.*" This means that God enlightens us through our human spirits. It also means that God reveals the unknown to us through our spirits.

PURPOSE IS DISCOVERED BY REVELATION

Another truth we can deduce from the response of Jesus is that the only person who can give true, accurate, and reliable information about the purpose of your life is God who is your Creator.

1 Corinthians 2:9-11, (The Voice), sheds a more detailed light on the process of divine revelation by stating:

But as the Scriptures say, No eye has ever seen and no ear has ever heard and it has never occurred to the human heart. All the things God prepared for those who love Him. God has shown us these profound and startling realities through His Spirit. The Spirit searches all things, even the deep mysteries of God.

There are profound and startling realities about your life that cannot be discovered through the human senses. They cannot be searched out using even the most sophisticated human equipment.

As said earlier, the purpose of a product is in the mind of the manufacturer. In this case, God is your Creator and the purpose of your life is hidden in His mind.

In spite of all the human sophisticated technology, there are planes and submarines lost in the vast ocean that we cannot even find. How much more will we find the mysteries hidden deep in the heart of God?

God's riches, wisdom, and knowledge are so deep that it is impossible to explain his decisions or to understand his ways - **(Romans 11:33, GW).**

The information classified as *"the deep things of God"* **(1 Corinthians 2:10)**, is beyond what anyone can search or dig out.

That is why **Deuteronomy 29:29, (NLT)** says:

The Lord our God HAS SECRETS KNOWN TO NO ONE. We are not accountable for them, but we and our children are accountable forever for all that he has REVEALED to us, so that we may obey all the terms of these instructions.

1 Corinthians 2:10 -12 (NLT) says:

But it was to us that God REVEALED these things BY HIS SPIRIT. For his Spirit searches out everything and SHOWS US GOD'S DEEP SECRETS.

No one can know a person's thoughts except that person's own spirit and no one can know God's thoughts except God's own Spirit. WE HAVE RECEIVED GOD'S SPIRIT (not the world's spirit), SO WE CAN KNOW the wonderful things God has freely given us.

If God can reveal the true and authentic identity of Jesus Christ to Peter then He can, and He will reveal your true identity to you. No human scheme, equipment or experiment can help you discover your true purpose and identity.

HOW TO DISCOVER YOUR TRUE IDENTITY

The secret to receiving divine wisdom and revelation was given in the book of James:

PURPOSE IS DISCOVERED BY REVELATION

If any of you LACKS WISDOM, you should ASK GOD, who gives generously to all without finding fault, and IT WILL BE GIVEN TO YOU.

But when you ask, you must believe and not doubt, because the one who doubts is like a wave of the sea, blown and tossed by the wind. That person should not expect to receive anything from the Lord. - (James 1:5- 7, NLT).

On the basis of this promise, you too can pray and ask God to reveal to you His purpose for your life. God will surely answer your prayer when you pray in faith, and you are expectant.

At this point, I bring to your attention that based on life and biblical evidences; people do get it wrong as far as their life purpose is concerned if there is no divine revelation from God. Most of the time, parents, siblings, teachers or people whose opinions are very important to you might actually be incorrect as far as your life purpose is concerned.

1. JEREMIAH

We earlier saw how Jeremiah **(Jeremiah 5:1-5)** argued with God that he was too young and did not possess the qualities to be who God said he was created to be.

2. DAVID

Another example was David whose king and brothers never believed he had the ability to fight and conquer Goliath **(1 Samuel 16)**. Furthermore, not even David's father felt he was good enough. At the time when the new king of Israel was to be appointed and anointed, Jesse, David's father, left him in the field to tend the sheep. He did not see in him the qualities required to hold the distinguished position of the next king of Israel. Even Samuel, the great prophet in Israel misjudged and almost anointed the wrong person as the new king. It took a divine REVELATION from God for Samuel not to commit the error.

Many times, we misjudge our potentials and what we are capable of accomplishing. You have far greater potential than what you think. That is why you should not let fear and limiting beliefs stop you from becoming the best you can be.

Most of the time, without God's revelation, people's opinions of your identity and capabilities will be wrong. Do not let other people's opinions become your fact.

3. JOSEPH

The brothers of Joseph did not have an understanding of God's divine purpose for him. So, rather than support him to achieve his divine assignment, they became obstacles. They devised an evil plan and sold Joseph as a slave. He was taken far away from home to Egypt by the slave traders. Interestingly, the actions that were intended to stop Joseph were the very ones that pushed him closer to the fulfillment of his purpose.

Right now, you may be in the same situation as Joseph was. The people you expected to support and encourage you in fulfilling your life calling might actually become the major stumbling blocks. Those who are supposed to be bridges may be towering walls. The great news is that no one, except you, can stop God's plan and purposes for your life.

One of the powerful mysteries of divine purpose is revealed in **Romans 8: 28 (NLT).**

And WE KNOW that GOD CAUSES EVERYTHING TO WORK TOGETHER for the good of those who love God and are called according to HIS PURPOSE for them

The understanding of this mystery will help you view life challenges and oppositions in a new light. It will take you through life's challenges with a positive attitude. It will save you from the spirit of bitterness and resentment.

The above scripture shows that God is actively working behind the scenes to make sure every experience of your life (good or bad) produces an ultimate, positive outcome.

So no matter what you are currently experiencing, you need to start focusing on the BIGGER picture: the ultimate purpose and outcome, which God promises to make good for you.

I know the plans that I have for you, declares the LORD. They are plans for peace and not disaster plans to give you a future filled with hope
- **(Jeremiah 29:11).**

4. JOHN THE BAPTIST.
God sent His angels to tell Zechariah he would have a boy child and his name should be called John.

Zechariah became deaf and dumb because he did not believe the words of the angel.

On the day the child was going to be named, Zechariah and his family gathered together to name the baby Zechariah after his father. Although their intentions were good from a human perspective, they were contrary to the instruction God gave to Zechariah.

This is a perfect example of a good and noble intention, which does not automatically translate to God's divine plan for your life.

The good can be the enemy of the best.

5. JESUS CHRIST

There was so much confusion and misconception as far as Jesus' purpose was concerned. Some called Him Isaiah; some called Him Jeremiah and others who did not know which name to call Him concluded that He was just one of the prophets. Some people even called Him King of the Jews. Moreover, even at a point, John the Baptist who introduced Jesus as the promised Messiah became doubtful and confused about who Jesus was and what his mission was.

While John was in the prison as a result of his arrest by Herod, he sent his disciples to Jesus to ask Him if He was the REAL promised Messiah or should they expect another one **(Luke 7:19).**

As human beings, we cannot fathom what God had in mind when He created us.

My ways are not your ways and my thoughts are not your thought, as the heaven are higher that the earth, so is my way and my thoughts higher that yours - **(Isaiah 55: 8).**

The foolishness of God is wiser than the best of human wisdom of mankind **(1 Corinthians 1:25).**

Isaiah 40:28 says that the understanding of God is too deep, and it is unsearchable.

All of these scriptures are meant to establish the truth that your life's purpose can only be discovered by divine revelation. You cannot experiment or research yourself into finding it.

The secret things belong to the LORD our God, but the things revealed belong to us and to our children forever, that we may follow all the words of this law - **(Deuteronomy 29:29).**

You might not have discovered your purpose yet. Also, no person might be able to tell you specifically what your purpose is. However, one thing that is certain is that you are a solution to someone or some people's problems. Everything God has created is a solution provider. The eyes are created to see; the hands are created to hold and touch and the legs are created to stand and to move around.

God Left You With Some Clues.

Now, concerning our life purposes, God has not left us in complete darkness. He has given us gifts, potentials, and passions as indicators of His plan and purposes for our lives.

The big challenge is that spiritually, there is a disconnection between mankind and God, so He gave us indicators by which we can have a glimpse of His eternal plan for our lives. Because of the separation between man and God, He needed to connect to us from the physical dimension through Jesus Christ so the broken relationship and the communication line between us and Him can be fixed.

In the meantime, before this spiritual communication line could be fixed, God devised the means for us to know about His existence using nature.

The spiritual and invisible God communicated to mankind about His existence and purpose using the physical things that we can perceive through our physical senses. In the same way, He uses our natural abilities, personalities, passions and our life experiences as guideposts to point us in the direction of our life callings.

Romans 1:20 gives us great insight into God's devised method of communicating with us while we are separated from Him and cannot receive spiritual revelations from Him. God "broadcasts" spiritual truths as revelations through the "transmitter" of the Holy Spirit.

No eye has seen, no ear has heard, no heart has imagined, what God has prepared for those who love Him." But God has revealed it to us by the Spirit **(1 Corinthians 2:9 – 10).**

And because only the deep calls to the deep, the revelations of God that are transmitted by the Spirit of God cannot be received or "perceived" by equipment of the physical senses.

That is why **1 Corinthians 2:14** says:
The natural man does not accept the things that come from the Spirit of God for they are foolishness to him, and he cannot understand them because they are spiritually discerned.

So in wisdom, God decided to communicate to us through the physical nature – the language we can understand.

Romans 1:20 (NLT) says:
For ever since the world was created, people have seen the earth and sky. Through everything God made, they can clearly see His invisible qualities – His eternal power and divine nature. So they have no excuse for not knowing God

What this scripture means in the context of the principle of this chapter is that if you take a careful look at a product and what it is capable of doing, what you will discover can give you an insight into what the product was created to do.

That is why the design of the hand is different from the design of the leg; they have different functions. Likewise, the design of the heart is different from the design of the lungs. So take a careful look at yourself, your gifts and talents (what you are good at doing) and your passion, (what you love and enjoy doing). Each one of these components is like a piece of the jigsaw puzzle called Purpose!

The Four Indicators of Purpose

You can start figuring out what was in the mind of God when He created you. There are four important components in your life that are God-given indicators of your purpose. These were meant to be God's revelation to mankind who are spiritually disconnected from God and cannot be enlightened by the Spirit of God through the human spirit. These components are:

1. Your Personality

2. Your Potential

3. Your Passion.

The combination of these three inbuilt indicators that God has put in place will give you some insight into what your life purpose is.

For since the creation of the world God's invisible qualities--his eternal power and divine nature--have been clearly seen, being understood from what has been made, so that people are without excuse.- **Romans 1:20 (NIV)**

4. Your Life Experiences

The fourth indicators of your life calling are the experiences and challenges of life that God has taken you through.

Rick Warren says that:
"God does not waste your hurt or pain. Your greatest ministry will flow out of your pain — not out of your

strengths or your talents but out of the painful experiences of your life. It is your weaknesses that help other people in their need, not your strengths."

2 Corinthians 1:2-5 (CEV) says:

I pray that God our Father and the Lord Jesus Christ will be kind to you and will bless you with peace! Praise God, the Father of our Lord Jesus Christ! The Father is a merciful God, who always gives us comfort. He comforts us when we are in trouble, so that we can share that same comfort with others in trouble. We share in the terrible sufferings of Christ, but also in the wonderful comfort he gives

Rick Warren also said:

"Who can be more sympathetic than somebody who has already been through what another person is going through right now? Who can better help the parent of a special needs child than a parent who raised a special needs child? Who can better help somebody going through a bankruptcy than somebody who has gone through it before? Who can better help somebody experiencing the heartbreak of divorce than somebody who remembers how terrible it felt? Who can better help somebody who's been abused or molested than somebody who has been abused or molested?"

If life hands you lemon, turn it to lemonade and invite the thirsty world to come and drink from the best lemonade ever.

The Limitation of Physical Revelation
God has prepared so much to do in and through your

life. What He has planned cannot be completely reduced to what the physical sense can perceive.

That is why the scripture says in **1 Corinthians 2:9:** *No eye has seen, no ear has heard, and no mind has imagined what God has prepared for those who love him.*

So a person who is not born again does not have his or her spirit renewed and awakened. Such a person is not in a relationship with God. The spirit of such an individual cannot be receptive to the communication and revelation of the Spirit of God.

Such people will be missing out on so many things related to life's callings and possibilities. They will be restricted to what they can perceive through the limited five senses and their thinking abilities.

Inexhaustible Resource is Available in Christ

There is an inexhaustible realm of wisdom, vision, and power in God that is made available to us when we are connected to Him through Christ Jesus.

God said in **Isaiah 55:8** that:
My thoughts are nothing like your thoughts, says the LORD. "And my ways are FAR BEYOND anything you could imagine. For just as the heavens are higher than the earth, so my ways are higher than your ways and my thoughts higher than your thoughts.

In order for you to be able to access and enjoy this inexhaustible resource and blessings that are made available in Christ through the power of the Holy Spirit, you will need to accept Jesus Christ into your life as your personal Lord and saviour.

PRINCIPLE #6
NOT EVERY PURPOSE IS KNOWN

They do not know or understand; they wander in darkness. All the foundations of the earth are shaken. I said, "You are gods; you are all sons of the Most High. However, you will die like men and fall like any other ruler - **(Psalm 82:5, HCSB)**

The meaning of the above scripture is that it is possible for people to be ignorant of their real identities. It also means that when you are not aware of your true identity, you will likely live below your capabilities and potential. The preceding scripture is directed to a people who are said to have the capabilities of gods but are dying like ordinary human beings because they do not understand the full extent of their power and potentials.

There are great challenges that are related to the ignorance of identity and life calling.

1. Self-Ignorance

2. People Ignorance

Self-Ignorance is when you are unaware of your life's calling or purpose. People ignorance is when the people around you cannot understand or perceive your gift and calling.

For example, if we look at the life of Jesus, we will realise that He was fully aware of who He was and what His assignment was. Yet, He faced a lot of opposition from the religious leaders of His day because they did not have a revelation of who He was and what His assignment was. Different people seem to have different ideas about who Jesus is. Some even called Him prince of demons because He was casting out devils. On the other hand, some people called Him the King of the Jews.

The religious leaders in the days of Jesus became very angry with Him when He said, *"Before Abraham was I am"* - (John 8:58). They actually concluded that he was either possessed by demons or he was mentally deranged.

21 Plagues of a Purposeless Life

Listed below are some of the possible effects of being ignorant of your life purpose and calling. I call the *21 Plagues of a Purposeless Life.*

1. Life will have no meaning.

2. Activities will become routine and burdensome.

3. Reduced ability to stay disciplined in life

4. Involvement in social vices.

5. Victim of peer pressure

6. Loss of identity or identity confusion
7. Comparison and competitiveness

8. Jealousy and resentment

9. Living by trial and error

10. Inability to be persistent in the face of opposition

11. Misplacement of priorities

12. Unduly seeking attention

13. Low self-esteem

14. Covering up fragile self-esteem with aggression or flashy fashion styles

15. Unstable and tosses to and fro by people's opinions

16. Lack of focus

17. Inability to manage relationships

18. Inability to cope with failure

19. Loss of peace and happiness

20. Depression

21. Suicide ideation or act of suicide

Understanding your identity, purpose, and life calling is an indispensable asset to both adults and children in the modern world. We now live in a world where there is much bullying, shaming, name-calling, and negative labeling. If you are unable to define who you are, the world will give you a definition and a label that is not your own.

In the scripture, there are quite a few people who were misjudged or misunderstood by their families, leaders or by the society at large. For example, the Jews did not understand the assignment of Jesus as the Messiah because they were expecting a warrior-Messiah who would physically engage the Roman army in an ultimate battle.

At some point, the religious leaders approached John the Baptist and asked him to define who he was and his reason for baptising people in the water. John was very bold and confident, even in the face of death because he understood who he was, why he was doing what he did and who sent him to do it.

I want you to carefully read below, the conversation of John the Baptist with the religious leaders who engaged him.

Contained in the conversation are very important lessons on why you should have the knowledge of your life calling and your purpose.

John 1:19-34:

This was John's testimony when the Jewish leaders sent priests and Temple assistants from Jerusalem to ask John, "Who are you?"

He came right out and said, "I am not the Messiah."

"Well then, who are you?" they asked. "Are you Elijah?" "No," he replied.

"Are you the Prophet we are expecting?" "No."

"Then who are you? We need an answer for those who sent us. What do you have to say about yourself?"

John replied in the words of the prophet Isaiah: "I am a voice shouting in the wilderness, 'Clear the way for the Lord's coming!'"

Then the Pharisees who had been sent asked him, "If you aren't the Messiah or Elijah or the Prophet, what right do you have to baptize?" John told them, "I baptize with water, but right here in the crowd is someone you do not recognize. Though his ministry follows mine, I'm not even worthy to be his slave and untie the straps of his sandal."

This encounter took place in Bethany, an area east of the Jordan River, where John was baptizing.

The next day John saw Jesus coming toward him and said, "Look! The Lamb of God who takes away the sin of the world!

He is the one I was talking about when I said, 'A man is coming after me who is far greater than I am, for he existed long before me.' I did not recognize him as the Messiah, but I HAVE BEEN BAPTIZING WITH WATER SO THAT HE MIGHT BE REVEALED TO ISRAEL."

Then John testified, "I saw the Holy Spirit descending like a dove from heaven and resting upon him. I didn't know he was the one, but when GOD SENT ME TO BAPTIZE WITH WATER, he told me, 'The one on whom you see the Spirit descend and rest is the one who will baptize with the Holy Spirit.' I saw this happen to Jesus, so I testify that he is the Chosen One of God.

Below is the list of the important information that John the Baptist knew about himself:

1. He knew who he was
2. He knew who he was not
3. He knew that he was sent
4. He knew who sent him
5. He knew who he was sent to
6. He knew why he was sent to Jesus
7. He knew why he was sent to baptise

If you look at the words of John the Baptist, you will notice that he was a man who was free from what I called *The 21 Plagues of Purposeless Life.*

John the Baptist knew that Jesus' ministry was greater than his ministry, and he was not ashamed to openly profess it. He was not in competition with Jesus; rather, he pointed people to Jesus.

His assignment was to make people look up to Jesus. He knew his calling and he celebrated his calling.

There was a time when the followers of John were about to pitch him against Jesus and sow seeds of competition and resentment, but John demonstrated an excellent attitude. He had the characteristics of someone who knew his gifting and was secure in his calling. John the Baptist was a man who did not allow the seed of insecurity and jealousy to create bitterness and resentment in him.

John 3:25-30 (ERV)

Some of John's followers had an argument with another Jew about religious washing. Then they came to John and said, "Teacher, remember the man who was with you on the other side of the Jordan River? He is the one you were telling everyone about. He is also baptizing people, and many are going to him."

John answered, "A person can receive only what God gives. You yourselves heard me say, 'I am not the Messiah. I am only the one God sent to prepare the way for him.' The bride always belongs to the bridegroom. The friend who helps the bridegroom just waits and listens. He is happy just to hear the bridegroom talk. That's how I feel now. I AM SO HAPPY that he is here. He must become more and more important, and I must become less important.

How many people are happy when others are progressing with their lives? How many leaders are willing to endorse another leader's gifting and potential? How many leaders are ready to give other people the needed push to become all they are created to be? How many leaders can be immune to the spirit of jealousy and competition?

If you are aware of your unique gifts and embrace your calling, you will live life peacefully and securely. You will also be immune to *the 21 Plagues of a Purposeless Life.*

PRINCIPLE #7

WHERE PURPOSE IS NOT KNOWN ABUSE IS INEVITABLE

The trees set out to anoint a king to rule them.

They said to the olive tree, "Reign over us." But the olive tree said to them, "Should I stop giving my oil that honours both God and man, and rule over the trees?"

Then the trees said to the fig tree, "Come and reign over us." But the fig tree said to them, "Should I stop giving my sweetness and my good fruit, and rule over trees?"

Later, the trees said to the grapevine, "Come and reign over us." But the grapevine said to them, "Should I stop giving my wine that cheers both God and man, and rule over trees?"

Finally, all the trees said to the bramble, "Come and reign over us." The bramble said to the trees, "If you really are anointing me as king over you, come and find refuge in my shade But if not, may fire come out from the bramble and consume the cedars of Lebanon - ***(Judges 9:8-15, HCSB).***

ABUSE MEANS ABnormal USE.

If you don't know or understand the purpose of your life, you are most likely putting your life to abnormal use or the wrong use. When people around you do not understand the purpose of your life, they often tend to misjudge or misguide you into following the wrong dream in life.

David was a young man who was never supported by his family. We saw earlier how he was not invited to the special meeting where the next king of Israel was going to be chosen and anointed. He was absent because those around him felt his presence at the meeting was unnecessary. But God thought differently.

That is why you should not allow other people's opinions of you to become what you believe about yourself. The common experience is that those close to you have gotten so used to you such that they can no longer recognise or appreciate your uniqueness.

It is ironic that at the meeting where David was not invited, he was, indeed, the most important person necessary for that meeting to be held. That is why he wrote in **Psalm 118:22** that: *The stone the builders have rejected has become the chief cornerstone.* After God revealed His intentions to Samuel, David, who was the key to God's plan, had to be hurriedly brought into the meeting and was anointed. Despite the opinion of the people close to David, he went on to become the greatest warrior-king Israel has ever had.

God said in **1 Samuel 13:14** that David was a man after His heart. In **Psalm 78: 72**, we are told that David *led Israel with the integrity of his heart and the skillfulness of his hand.*

When David was going to fight Goliath in **1 Samuel 16**, His brothers were one of the first set of people who antagonized him and undermined his ability to face Goliath. But he did not allow other people's opinions to stop him from pursuing what he believed was his life calling and divine assignment.

Another familiar example was Joseph whose brothers did not only despise him, but they also took strategic steps to sabotage his life dreams.

Some people can do the most unusual and unimaginable things to stop you when they do not understand the purpose of your life. No one can see the dream and feel the passion that God has placed in your heart.

All the different kinds of abuses in our world are the result of a lack of understanding about purpose. However, God's Word teaches us how much He values the weak and ordinary people that abused or neglected.

Type of Abuses --- What God's Word Says:

Child abuse - Children are God's heritage
(Psalm 127:3)

Sex abuse - Marriage is honourable the bed undefiled (Hebrews 13:4)

Marriage abuse - Wives, submit yourselves to your own husbands. Husbands, love your wives (Ephesians 5:22,25).

Abuse of position
of authority -   A person who wants to be the head must be servant of all. (Matthew 20:26)

Comparing Kids

Some parents and teachers have a habit of comparing kids. They do so because they are ignorant of the fact that purposes and gifting are different. A teacher once sent Thomas Edison home after three months in school saying he was too dull to learn. He went on to become one of the greatest inventors who ever lived.

Les Brown, *a world-class motivational speaker,* also shared his experience in school when he was labeled as a slow learner. That marker formed his identity and hindered his ability to learn until another teacher told him: *"Don't let another person's opinion about you become your fact about yourself."*

A lot of people are being held back from fulfilling their potentials and pursuing their dreams because of other people's limiting opinions about them or their own restricted thoughts about themselves. Many people are locked into professions or businesses that are inconsistent with their passions and potentials because of other people's opinions. We need to remind ourselves **that where purpose is not known, abnormal use is inevitable.**

Another form of exposing your life to abnormal use is engaging in activities that are outside the scope of your gifting or calling. When you are not doing what you were created to do and not fitted for you, it's like trying to place a round peg in a square hole. You have an inner uneasiness that yearns for satisfaction. You lack peace deep down within. Great potential is locked in because where you are, does not provide the platform for the expression of those potentials. Therefore, location is of utmost importance in life.

Unless a grain of wheat falls into the earth and dies, it remains alone; but if it dies, it bears much fruit - **(John 12:24).**

You might be in a wrong location or engaged in the wrong life activity that is not providing the right environment for your life to be unraveled and the potential in you to be unleashed. Destiny can be magnified or limited depending on location. Except a seed finds the right environment, it will remain as a single seed, despite the capability for increase that is locked within it.

We are all like seeds in God's hand with unprecedented levels of potential. David said: *Thank you for making me so wonderfully complex! Your workmanship is marvelous* - **(Psalm 139:14, NLT).**

Do not settle for what is available. Rather, seek out and locate the right environment for your potential, then go ahead and bury yourself (by dogged focus and commitment) into what God has created you to do. Then and only then can you *"bring forth much fruits."*

PRINCIPLE #8
EVERY PURPOSE HAS ITS TIME AND SEASON

To everything there is a season, and a time to every purpose under the heaven - **(Ecclesiastes 3:1).**

LIFE IS IN SEASONS

In the Chapter 1 of this book, I explained the difference between time and eternity. I also made mention of the fact that time is measurable and it has a beginning and an end point.

Life's purpose is an assignment that is given which is meant to be completed within a specified period of time.

That is to say that every purpose here on earth has a time period assigned to it. A goal is just a dream without a deadline.

In **John 9:4**, Jesus said: *I must do the work of him that sent me while it is day for night is coming when no one can work.*

The fundamental truth expressed in this scripture is that you have a specified period within which you are expected to accomplish your purpose.

Once the spirit and soul depart from the body, the work of a person here on earth ceases, whether they have completed it or not. There is a difference between ceasing from your work because of death and transitioning to glory because your work is completed.

The difference between the two can be illustrated by the example of a student sitting an examination. Every examination usually comes with an allotted time. The exam may come to an end because the time allotted is completed. However, it does not necessarily mean the all the exam questions have been attempted.

In the case of Jesus Christ, it was written that when He realised all the requirements on Earth and on the cross were completed He said, "It is finished" and then He gave up His Spirit. (John 19:29 - 30)

We also have the example of Paul who said in:

2 Timothy 4: 7, *I have finished my course, I have kept the faith. I am ready to be poured out like an offering.*

The concepts behind this principle are:

1. God decides your purpose.

2. He determines the gifts and talents you required to fulfill the purpose.

3. He determines the time frame required to finish the assignment.

4. He then designs and creates, giving us the potentials required to fulfill the purpose within the

allotted period of time. In His wisdom, He also factors in the detours in our lives.

David wrote:

Your eyes saw me when I was inside the womb. All the DAYS ORDAINED FOR ME were recorded in your scroll BEFORE one of them came into existence **- (Psalm 139:16, NET).**

We all have a specific number of days (lifespan) allotted or given to us. This is what Jesus referred to as "daytime." Once that time period is over, the night time comes. Once the period of time allotted to a person is over, he or she enters the "night" period and ceases from ALL works.

Below are two powerful but related quotes that I will like to share with you as related to fulfilling the purpose and dreams that God has planted in your heart:

"The graveyard is the richest place on earth, because it is here that you will find all the hopes and dreams that were never fulfilled, the books that were never written, the songs that were never sung, the inventions that were never shared, the cures that were never discovered, all because someone was too afraid to take that first step, keep with the problem, or determined to carry out their dream"
- (Les Brown).

The next quote is from **Myles Munroe**, of blessed memory:

"The wealthiest places in the world are not gold mines, oil fields, diamond mines or banks. The

wealthiest place is the cemetery. There lies companies that were never started, masterpieces that were never painted... In the cemetery there is buried the greatest treasure of untapped potential. There is a treasure within you that must come out. Don't go to the grave with your treasure still within YOU"
- **(Myles Munroe).**

What visions and dreams have you not accomplished because of procrastination? Maybe you are waiting for the perfect time. Maybe you are waiting for more money. Or you are waiting for the approval of family and friends, which might never come. Maybe self-doubt is holding you back. Are you being held back by a sense of insecurity?

Are you waiting for someone to motivate you to do what you know you ought to do? I need to let you know that self-motivation is the best motivation because the person you are waiting for may never show up.

"Motivation is what gets you started. Habit is what keeps you going" - **(Jim Rohn).**

Don't forget there is a time and a season for EVERY PURPOSE and that a PURPOSE is beautiful in its SEASON.

It will be a tragedy of life if you allow the time allotted to you to elapse while you are still waiting for the "right time" to execute those dreams in your heart.

Jesus said in **John 4:34:** *My nourishment is to DO THE WILL OF HIM WHO SENT ME and to FINISH the work he has given me.*

That was Jesus' life's pledge to himself – to DO and to FINISH the assignment he has been given.

What is your own personal pledge to yourself about your life's calling?

PRINCIPLE #9
PURPOSE DETERMINES POTENTIALS

The LORD has gifted Bezalel, Oholiab, and the other skilled craftsmen with wisdom and ability to perform any task involved in building the sanctuary. Let them construct and furnish the Tabernacle, just as the LORD has commanded - **(Exodus 36:1).**

PURPOSE COMES WITH TOOLS

What are potentials? Your potentials are the natural, inborn gifts and talents that you have. They enable you to do some specific things very well and with little difficulty. They are so natural you don't struggle to excel in the area of your potential.

For example, if you have the talent to sing, you will notice that singing just comes naturally to you. If you have the talent to draw, drawing objects or images can be so easy that people around you marvel at the ease with which you do such beautiful works of art. If you are gifted with creative imagination, producing work of inventions will be second nature to you.

Potentials are part of the many resources given to you by God to enable you to fulfill your purpose. That is why I mentioned in the earlier chapters that your potential is one of the indicators to your God-given purpose What you do well or you are naturally good at doing can give you some insight into the purpose of God for your life.

In the book of **Exodus 31: 2-6 (NLT)** God said to Moses:

Look, I have SPECIFICALLY CHOSEN Bezalel son of Uri, grandson of Hur, of the tribe of Judah. I have FILLED HIM with the Spirit of God, giving him GREAT WISDOM, ability, and expertise in all kinds of crafts. He is a master craftsman, expert in working with gold, silver, and bronze. He is skilled in engraving and mounting gemstones and in carving wood. He is a master at every craft!

And I have PERSONALLY APPOINTED Oholiab son of Ahisamach, of the tribe of Dan, to be his assistant. Moreover, I have given SPECIAL SKILL to all the gifted craftsmen SO THEY CAN MAKE all the things I have commanded you to make.

Bezalel and Oholiab were specifically chosen and gifted by God to make artistic designs. They were to lead other craftsmen in the making of the artwork for the Ark of the Covenant. As a result of this choice and assignment, God gave them wisdom and skills in all kinds of craft.

We can see from this story that God chooses and empowers you for your specific assignment.

PURPOSE DETERMINES POTENTIALS

Bezalel and Oholiab were given gifts and skills to create art and craft because that is what they needed to fulfil their assignment.

Another great lesson from this story is that your gift is a guidepost to your purpose and calling. Gifts, talents, and potentials were not given at random. Principle #1 says that *"There is a Purposeful Creator."*

The principle in this chapter says that: *Purpose Determines Potential.*

There are different types of gifts and talents. Every gift, talent, and potential comes from God. God is the one who determines and decides who gets what gifts. This is not a human decision but a divine one. Gifts and talents are given to each to enable them to fulfil their divine purpose and in the process, benefit mankind. So we can say with every assurance that it is your purpose that determines the kind of potential that you are given. This is because your potential is a tool or resource to fulfil your purpose.

In the Bible, we have examples of how this principle played out in the lives of different Bible characters.

1. DAVID

David was a warrior-leader. He was naturally a fearless person. The enemy that made the best of soldiers afraid made the fearless warrior in David come alive (1 Samuel 17: 10-11, 23-24, 26, 32).

2. JOSEPH

Joseph had the gift of interpreting dreams. Dreaming and interpreting dreams came naturally to Joseph from the time he was a young boy. This gift became a major tool used by God to secure Joseph's freedom and give him a position of relevance in a strange country.

The gifts of Joseph did cut through the barrier of citizenship requirements, and he became the prime minister in Egypt. **Proverbs 18:16** says, *The gift of a person will make way for him and lead him into the presence of great people.*

The gift of Joseph helped him secure a prime position in Egypt and that position helped him to fulfil the assignment of saving lives during the time of great famine in the world.

In **Genesis 45: 7**, Joseph told his brothers, who sold him into slavery: *God sent me ahead of you to keep you and your families and to preserve many survivors.*

3. SAMSON

Samson was a man of extraordinary human strength. He was born with a specific assignment to be a leader who would defend and deliver the Israelites from their enemies. The strategy of Samson was to be a one-man army. So God gifted him with extraordinary physical strength.

In **Judges 15:16**, Samson took on the entire Philistine's army, all by himself, with just the jaw bone of a donkey; he killed a thousand Philistines.

This kind of extraordinary human ability was required at that time by Samson in order for him to fulfill his God-given assignment.

From these examples, we can understand that God decides our purposes and our assignments, He then goes ahead to give us the gifts and talents we require as tools to fulfill our purposes.

THE MAN WITH A WOMB

This is a reference to a woman as being a man with a womb (WOmb Man). A womb is a tool of purpose that God has given to a woman to enable her to fulfill her assignment of childbearing. God also gave women breasts so they can nurture their babies.

When we understand and believe in the principle of purpose, we will come to a realization that gender reassignment is a major life issue.

It is like manufacturing an aircraft and later deciding to change it to a Mercedes Benz car or manufacturing a bus and later deciding to change it to a car. No matter how we try to explain it away, it is a fundamental life and purpose issue. Changing an iPhone 5 to an iPhone 6 or vice versa might not be a project that an Apple's techies will be so excited to embark on.

For ever since the world was created, people have seen the earth and sky. Through everything God made, they can clearly see his invisible qualities--his eternal power and divine nature. So they have no excuse for not knowing God - **(Romans 1:20).**

The direct interpretation of this passage is that the work of God, His creation, and workmanship help us understand the nature and quality of the God who created all those things.

When you observe the work of an artist you can understand so much about the artists, her skill, and taste without even meeting her in person.

Now to apply that passage to the principle in this chapter, we can say that when we carefully observe a person, his or her personality, potential, passion, background, culture, gender and all other inborn natural characteristics, we can begin to piece together the thought in the mind of the person who created him or her.

Just as God revealed Himself through nature He has also revealed Himself and His purpose for your life through your nature (personality) and talent.

PRINCIPLE #10
PURPOSE DETERMINES PROVISION

When I sent you without purse and script, did you lack anything? - **(Luke 22:35)**

FOR EVERY VISION THERE IS A PROVISION

Your purpose and your assignment will determine the kind and level of provision that will be made available to you. God provides human and material resources for you to facilitate the accomplishment of the assignment He has given you. Whatever you require to accomplish your assignment, God will provide.

In **Luke 22: 35**, Jesus asked His disciples: *When I sent you without purse and script, did you lack anything?*

In **Hebrew 6:5** Jesus Christ said: *A body has been prepared for me.*

Jesus needed a physical body when He came down from heaven, so He could operate here on earth. He also needed a physical body to withstand the excruciating stress of going on the cross to accomplish the assignment of being our sacrificial Lamb.

The tools and resources that you need to fulfil your destiny have been prepared for you, and they will manifest at the appointed time. That is why the journey of purpose is journey of faith. You don't wait for resources BEFORE you step out. Rather, you step out being fully persuaded that the resources have been provided and they will manifest at the appointed time.

In Genesis 22, God spoke to Abraham to make him a sacrifice.

While on the way to make the sacrifice commanded by God Isaac spoke up and said to his father, Abraham:

"Father?" "Yes, my son?" Abraham replied.

"The fire and wood are here," Isaac said, "but where is the lamb for the burnt offering?"

Abraham answered, "God himself will provide the lamb for the burnt offering, my son." And the two of them went on together - **(Genesis 22:8).**

You need to go on. Do not ever allow "lack of resources" to stop you from taking action.

THE MYSTERY LIFE OPPORTUNITIES

God Himself will divinely connect you to people, opportunities, and resources. For example, Ruth found her food supply and her husband in a place where she was working hard to support her mother-in-law (Ruth 1-4).

Your purpose and assignment will determine the *where* and the *when* of your supply.

In the time of great famine, God made provision for the supply required by Prophet Elijah

Leave here, turn eastward and hide by the brook of Cherith, I have Commanded the raven to FEED YOU THERE- **(1 King 17:3).**

God made a promise of consistent provision to Elijah, despite the famine. The only requirement necessary was that he should be rightly positioned. For as long as it was required, God provided food for Elijah through the raven and drink from the brook.

When the place of assignment shifted, the brook dried up and the raven stopped coming. That is why it is a lack of faith to be tied to an agent of divine supply or to be disappointed when supplies stop coming from an agent of supply.

God is your source, and He can decide to use whichever agent He chooses to meet your needs. Your life and ministry must never be tied to any agent of supply. God is your source and God's will is God's bill. God ALONE is your great supplier.

Although Elijah was getting comfortable with staying by the brook, God had an assignment for him somewhere else. At that time, there was a widow in a small town of Zarephath who was trusting God for a miracle supply to sustain her and her son through the great famine.

She was about to prepare her last meal because she had ran out of food. Then God sent Elijah to her as an agent of deliverance from the famine. Despite the fact that she was a widow, and she was on her last meal, God provided supplies for Elijah in Zarephath all through the period of famine. That was because the widow's house was a place of assignment for Elijah.

God can legitimately make provision for you from the most unlikely places and through the most unexpected people. Your responsibility to qualify is to be obedient and stay at the centre of His calling for your life.

God told Elijah:

Go at once to Zarephath in the region of Sidon and stay there. I have directed a widow there to supply you with food- **(1 Kings 17:9).**

PRINCIPLE #11
PURPOSES ARE INHERENT

YOUR PURPOSE IS CODED.
It is inborn, inbuilt, in-wired and in-coded into your DNA. Your Purpose is coded into every fibre of your cell, your being, your spirit, soul, and body.

This principle was clearly demonstrated in the life of Moses:

Many years later, when Moses had grown up, he went out to visit his own people, the Hebrews, and he saw how hard they were forced to work. During his visit, he saw an Egyptian beating one of his fellow Hebrews.

*After looking in all directions to make sure no one was watching, Moses killed the Egyptian and hid the body in the sand. - **(Exodus 2:11-12, NLT)**.*

Moses had always felt that his life's calling was to deliver Israel from their slavery in Egypt. But because of his limited understanding, he tried to accomplish it using the wrong method. This wrong method landed him in so much trouble such that he had to run away from Egypt like a fugitive.

Moses was about 40 years of age at the time he ran away from Egypt.

Fast forward 40 years later; God appeared to Moses and sent him to Egypt as His instrument of delivering Israel from their slave master.

Look! The cry of the people of Israel has reached me, and I have seen how harshly the Egyptians abuse them. Now go, for I am sending you to Pharaoh. You must lead my people Israel out of Egypt - **(Exodus 3:10-11).**

Exodus 2:11-12 shows that Moses had demonstrated a passionate to deliver the children of Israel from their Egyptian slave masters 40 years before he was called and sent by God.

There are certain visions, dreams, ideas, and passions that have stayed with you consistently since you were a kid, and they have never left you. Why did those vision and dreams stayed on with you? It is because God coded your calling and your assignment right within. **Romans 11:29 (NIV)** says that: *God's gifts and his call are irrevocable.*

Your life's calling and assignments determined the way you were designed and wired. The above scripture shows how important it is for you to stay in the place of your calling.

Then his disciples remembered this prophecy from the Scriptures: "Passion for God's house will consume me. -(John 2:17).

This is a reference to Jesus Christ and how He was driven by the passion for the calling of God on His life.

Another person whose life depicted this principle was Joseph the dreamer. Joseph had dreams of becoming a leader of great influence while he was just a kid. He later became the prime minister of Egypt. At the time when Joseph became the prime minister, Egypt was the most powerful and influential nation in the world.

The dreams God had planted in your heart might look impossible or far-fetched, but if you believe God and follow His leading, what crosses your mind will one day cross your path.

David's life also modeled this principle. David started his life as a young shepherd boy. The young shepherd boy discovered that he had a fearless spirit to confront wild animal that came to attack the flock he was looking after. He also had an unusual passion to defend the defenseless lambs that were under his care.

In 1 Samuel 17: 34, David gave an account of how he had to confront a lion and a bear while he was looking after his father's flock. He did so to save a lamb. Inherent in David was the gifting and the fighting spirit of a warrior leader. It was a fearless spirit against the enemy. It was the will that could not be defeated by the enemy. David later went on to become a warrior king in Israel.

Where you are right now might not be where you want to be, but if you apply the principle of "whatsoever your hands find to do , do it with all your heart" - (Ecclesiastes 9:10a Colossians 3:23), your present location might become the launching pad to your desired location.

David discovered and developed his talent in a place of obscurity by committing himself to the opportunity at hand. The obscure location became the breeding ground for his talents. It was the talents and passion that he developed in the place of obscurity that God used to announce him to the world.

Obscurity is not a curse. In the path way of purpose, obscurity is usually a "hideaway" in order to prepare for a "break away."

As a young boy without any military experience, David was courageous when he stepped forward to confront Goliath. He did so despite the fact that Goliath had an unusually great stature, advanced military skill and warfare experiences.

For forty days, Goliath challenged and harassed the army of Israel. He created an atmosphere of great fear within the camp of the Israelites. . No soldier or general in the Israelites' army was bold or confident enough to volunteer and face Goliath. Although the situation was desperate, not even Saul the king would volunteer.

When David saw Goliath and heard his threats, instead of being afraid, the inherent warrior-leader in him was awakened, and he volunteered to fight Goliath. Everyone thought that David did not have the skills and experience to fight Goliath.

David fearlessly confronted Goliath and brought him down just has he boldly promised.

What you love (e.g working with children), what you hate (e.g injustice), what moves you to tears (e.g human suffering), what motivates you to action, what gets you angry, what you are willing to confront, what gets your creative juices flowing etc., may be the indicators of your divine assignment.

It might be something the people around you cannot be bothered about but it keeps you awake all night. This happens because something in your inner being resonates with the very thing that is bothering you. You may have a calling to do something positive about it.

Because purpose is inbuilt, our passions usually stay with us all our lives. What you have always loved when you were young might not end up being the career you pursue but it will always be a place where you will derive fulfillment.

PRINCIPLE #12
YOUR BIRTH IS EVIDENCE THAT YOUR PURPOSE IS NECESSARY

Jesus replied, "You say that I am a king. For this reason I was born, and for this reason I came into the world--to testify to the truth. Everyone who belongs to the truth listens to my voice - **(John 18:37, NET).**

EVERYTHING AND EVERYONE GOD CREATED IS A PROBLEM SOLVER.

The hand can reach and touch; the leg allows movement; the eyes can see; the ears can hear. Every single part of the organs in our bodies was created to serve a particular function or solve a problem. There is no organ in human body that is without a function, no matter how minute and hidden away it might be.

You were not created just to add to the population of the world. You were created as a problem solver, as a healing balm to some wounds, as a light to some people's darkness. You are creates as salt to arrest decay and decadence and provide sweetness in some places in this world.

The bible says: *You are the salt of the earth. But what good is salt if it has lost its flavour? Can you make it salty again? It will be thrown out and trampled underfoot as worthless* - **(Matthew 5:13)**.

The power and importance of purpose are expressed by Jesus in the above scripture. Our purposes add value to our lives. When you lose your purpose and your function, you lose your value and your relevance.

Luke 8:16 says that: *No one lights a lamp and then covers it with a bowl or hides it under a bed. A lamp is placed on a stand, where its light can be seen by all who enter the house.*

In **Luke 8:16** Jesus shows the connection between you, the tools that are provided for you to fulfill your purpose (lampstands) and the assignment you have been given (to provide light).

This scripture says no man lights a candle and puts it under the bushel. The lighting of a candle signifies your birth. You were birthed for a reason. God is not in the business of creating "good for nothing" humans. The scripture assures us that God made the provision of the lampstands for you to be able to manifest your purpose.

The above scripture contains deep revelations to the fact that your birth proves your purpose is necessary. A person who has lost his or her vision to make contributions or solve problems is classified as having a "good for nothing" life. This is a strongly worded statement from the mouth of Jesus Himself.

This paints a clear picture of the great value God places on you fulfilling the purpose for which you were born.

We also discovered from this scripture that our glory and our relevance in life are realised when we manifest our purposes. People are not rewarded in life because of their age, colours or backgrounds but because of their contributions.

Just like in the case of Mary and baby Jesus, the bible made mention of the wise mean that came to visit and gave gifts to Jesus. According the scriptures, *They entered the house and saw the child with his mother, Mary, and they bowed down and worshiped him. Then they opened their treasure chests and gave HIM gifts of gold, frankincense, and myrrh -* **(Matthew 2:11, NLT).**

The wise men did not travel all the distance looking for Mary. They came looking for Jesus, who was Mary's contribution to mankind. They did not bow down to Mary or give their gifts to her. They gave their gifts to Jesus.

The contributions you make is your own "baby" that the world is waiting for. There is no great life – only great service, great sacrifice, and great contributions. A life is classified as great in the measure to which the person is manifesting the purpose for which they are created and fulfilling their God-given assignment.

Jesus referred to a life that is not making contributions or fulfilling the purpose for which it was created a "good for nothing" life. This also tells us that there is no life that does not have a capacity to make a contribution. There are people who are born with severe disabilities but who chose to use their disability to contribute inspiration to mankind. Such people took their lemon and tuned it to lemonade.

Change Impossible to I'm possible

Sparsh Shah Changed the word "Impossible" to "I'm Possible"

Sparsh Shah is an Indian-American who was born in Iselin, Middlesex in the state of New Jersey, United States on the 1st of May, 2003 with severe osteogenesis imperfecta (or brittle bone syndrome).

This syndrome is characterized by fragile bones that break easily.

- He came out of the womb with 35 bone fractures because of the brittle bone syndrome.

- In the first 14 years of his life, he has already had over 130 fractures.

But despite the fact that Sparsh is physically challenged with brittle bone syndrome, his spirit is unbreakable.

- He wrote his first song (with help from a friend) at the age of 6.

- He has now written 13 songs to date.

- He aspires to be a professional singer and start his own record-label one day.

- At the young age of 6, he was able to spell a 45-letter word in English: "Pneumonoultramicroscopicsilicovolcanoconiosis."

- He has performed at Madison Square Garden.

- He auditioned for season 12 of America's Got Talent.

- He gave a TED Talk.

In his very popular interview with PEOPLE Magazine (www.people.com), he said:

"I've gone through my share of rough spots in life, but I don't let it get to me. I want to show people that no matter what happens in your life, you should never ever give up on your passion, and mine is singing and creating music. I just feel like MY REASON FOR BEING IS TO SING. I was meant to sing and INSPIRE PEOPLE through my music and message.

I felt the power of music before I could even speak. My parents would put songs on the car speaker and I'd be humming along. SINGING IS A SPIRITUAL GIFT FROM GOD, because it allows me to express my feelings. There is so much beauty in singing, I want to inspire people. I think music was the CALLING that I got. IT'S MY LIFE'S CALLING: It is, it was and it always will be.

Look, people ask me what my dream or goal in life is, but I'm already living my dream. I'M DOING WHAT I WAS DESTINED TO DO.

But, I guess if I have a dream... it's to sing in front of 1 billion people one day.

[Teen with Brittle Bone Syndrome Brings NBA Crowd to Tears During National Anthem: Singing 'Allows Me to Express My Feelings' – **(www.people.com)**]

Sparsh Shah is such a great inspiration. Although I "stumbled" on his TEDx talk tagged: "How a 13-year-old changed 'Impossible' to 'I'm Possible.'" after I had finished the initial manuscript of this book, I found that his story is the 21 Principles of Purpose encapsulated.

There is nothing more exciting than to see someone living the 21 principles right before you.

Sparsh Shah discovered his inherent passion and gifting for music at age 6. He refused to allow his physical challenge to stop him from fulfilling his purpose. Rather, he turned his lemon to lemonade, and he is making a worldwide contribution through music and inspirational talks.

Irrespective of what you lack, what you think you don't have or the limitations you experience, the fact remains that your birth is evidence that there is a purpose for your life.

Your birth is evidence that you are needed and that some people are out there waiting for you to shine your light so they can see the pathways through their own situations.

Your light can be a word, a drawing, a poem, an article, a book, a song, a project, a vocation.

YOUR PURPOSE IS NECESSARY

Stop focusing on what you don't have or what you cannot do and start tapping into the possibilities inherent within you that are waiting to be tapped.

You too can change your mentality from "impossible" to "I'm possible" and a whole new level of possibilities will open up for you.

As a man thinks in his heart so is he. If you think you can then you can. If you think that you can't, then you can't.

The world is waiting for your contribution. Step out! Step up! Step forward and unleash the greatness within you.

PRINCIPLE #13
PURPOSE IS BOTH GENERAL AND SPECIFIC

For the same God who worked through Peter as the apostle to the Jews also worked through me as the apostle to the Gentiles - **(Galatians 2:8).**

THE SPECIFIC IS EMBEDDED IN THE GENERAL

In the above scripture, Paul affirms that the same God, who sent Peter to the Jews, sent him to the Gentiles.

Galatians 2:8 is very important and foundational to the principle in this chapter.

In Matthew 28:19 - 20, every believer is given the responsibility to preach the gospel just like Peter and Paul. The instruction to preach the gospel is a general instruction. Who the preaching should be directed towards is usually a specific instruction. Every message is directed to an individual or group of people. For example, Peter and Paul were sent to preach the gospel, but Peter was specifically sent to the Jews while Paul was specifically sent to the Gentiles.

Other examples are Moses and Aaron in the book of Exodus Chapter 3. Both of these men were sent by God as His agents to deliver the children of Israel from their Egyptian slave masters. The general assignment was to secure the freedom of the Israelites from Egypt, but the individual roles and tasks required to accomplish the assignment were different. God said Moses would be a god to Pharaoh and Aaron would be the mouth piece of Moses.

Note also that as the general purpose progresses, the specific roles and assignments advanced. For example, when they were in Egypt, Aaron was the mouth piece for Moses to communicate with Pharaoh. But when they were in the wilderness journeying to the Promise Land, the roles changed.

The stand was no longer between Moses and Pharaoh; rather it was between God and Israel. The office of the priest was created by God and He commanded that Aaron and his family should occupy that office to administer the sacrifices of Israel. Aaron went on to step into the exalted role of a high priest. This is a role that is different from being a priest. Priests present daily offerings on the altar of sacrifice for individuals and families. On the other hand, the high priest entered the Holy of Holies once a year to stand before the Ark of the Covenant making sacrifices for a whole nation.

PURPOSE IS BOTH GENERAL AND SPECIFIC

Aaron's life is a vivid example of the progressive nature of God's purpose in our lives.

Moses and Samuel were great leaders in Israel but never at any time did they lead Israel into battle. Joshua and David, on the other hand, led Israel's army to several victorious battles. Moses and Samuel were assigned by God as prophet-leaders while Joshua and David were warrior-leaders according to the assignments that God gave to them.

Saul missed these distinctions and it cost him his throne:

Meanwhile, Saul stayed at Gilgal, and his men were trembling with fear. Saul waited there seven days for Samuel, as Samuel had instructed him earlier, but Samuel still didn't come. Saul realized that his troops were rapidly slipping away. So he demanded, "Bring me the burnt offering and the peace offerings!" And Saul sacrificed the burnt offering himself

Just AS SAUL WAS FINISHING WITH THE BURNT OFFERING, SAMUEL ARRIVED. Saul went out to meet and welcome him, but Samuel said, "WHAT IS THIS YOU HAVE DONE?" Saul replied, "I saw my men scattering from me, and you didn't arrive when you said you would, and the Philistines are at Micmash ready for battle.

So I said, 'The Philistines are ready to march against us at Gilgal, and I haven't even asked for the Lord's help!' So I felt compelled TO OFFER THE

BURNT OFFERING MYSELF BEFORE YOU CAME."

"HOW FOOLISH!" Samuel exclaimed. "You have not kept the command the Lord your God gave you. Had you kept it, the Lord would have established your kingdom over Israel forever.

*BUT NOW YOUR KINGDOM MUST END, for the Lord has sought out a man after his own heart. The Lord has already appointed him to be the leader of his people, because you have not kept the Lord's command - **(1 Samuel 13:8 -14, NLT).***

Samson was also a warrior-leader but the specifics of his operation were different from those of David and Joshua. Samson was a one-man army of a sort. God gave him extraordinary human strength to confront the armies of the enemies.

As Samson arrived at Lehi, the Philistines came shouting in triumph. But the Spirit of the Lord came powerfully upon Samson, and he snapped the ropes on his arms as if they were burnt strands of flax, and they fell from his wrists.

Then he found the jawbone of a recently killed donkey. He picked it up and killed 1,000 Philistines with it. Then Samson said,

> *"With the jawbone of a donkey,*
> *I've piled them in heaps!*
> *With the jawbone of a donkey,*
> *I've killed a thousand men!"*

PURPOSE IS BOTH GENERAL AND SPECIFIC

When he finished his boasting, he threw away the jawbone; and the place was named Jawbone Hill. - (Judges 15: 14 - 17).

A final example for this chapter is the assignment that God gave to the Moon and the Sun after they were crated:

God made two great lights—the larger one to govern the day, and the smaller one to govern the night. He also made the stars. God set these lights in the sky to light the earth, to govern the day and night, and to separate the light from the darkness. And God saw that it was good - **(Genesis 1:16- 17, NLT).**

The sun and the Moon were both created to give light to the earth as a general purpose or assignment. But the specifics in terms of method, intensity, and timing were different. The sun was created and commanded to give light during the day when a light with greater intensity and warmth is mostly required. The moon was commanded to give its own light during the night when a light with less intensity is required so that we can sleep well.

The specifics of the assignment of the sun and the moon determined their design and location. The moon was created and positioned to reflect the light from the Sun to the earth. On the other hand, the Sun was created to be a very powerful source of light and warmth. It was also positioned to give just the right amount of light and warmth for the survival of life on the earth.

In your endeavour to fulfil your purpose, you will need to discover, not just your general purpose but also the specifics. This will prevent you from comparing yourself to others and following someone's style or method, which might be different from what you are created or equipped to do. Principles do not change, but styles, methods, and specifics of assignments may vary.

PRINCIPLE #14
NO PURPOSE IS BETTER THAN THE OTHER

I planted the seed in your hearts, and Apollos watered it, but it was God who made it grow - (1 Corinthians 3:6, NLT).

For the same God who worked through Peter as the apostle to the Jews also worked through me as the apostle to the Gentiles.
In fact, James, Peter, and John, who were known as pillars of the church, recognized the gift God had given me, and they accepted Barnabas and me as their co-workers - (Galatians 2:8-9).

But Jesus called them together and said, "You know that the rulers in this world lord it over their people, and officials flaunt their authority over those under them. But among you it will be different.

Whoever wants to be a leader among you must be your servant, and whoever wants to be first among you must become your slave
- (Matthew 20:25 - 27, NLT).

You are not better than me, and I am not better than you. You are the best for your purpose, and I am the best for mine. We are all uniquely different and equally valuable.

God is no respecter of persons, colour or nationality.

A careful study of the system of the human body gives us an understanding of this principle.

You are created for a purpose, which is like a piece of a big puzzle. The big puzzle represents the total plan and purpose of God for the universe, both in time and in eternity.

Our human body is made up of many unique organs. Each of these organs has its specific function and role. To have a healthy body, every cell and organ in it needs to perform their specific roles in harmony with other cells and organs.

In some cases where organ transplants are performed, the body sees a newly transplanted organ as a foreign object and unleashes antibodies to fight and kill it. Although the newly planted organ was supposed to work harmoniously with other organs in the body and so help the body to create a healthy body system, the wrong labeling incapacitates the organ from performing its function and roles.

Just as our bodies have many parts and each part has a special function, so it is with Christ's body. We are many parts of one body, and we all belong to each other.

NO PURPOSE IS BETTER THAN THE OTHER

In his grace, God has given us different gifts for doing certain things well. So if God has given you the ability to prophesy, speak out with as much faith as God has given you. If your gift is serving others, serve them well. If you are a teacher, teach well.

If your gift is to encourage others, be encouraging. If it is giving, give generously. If God has given you leadership ability, take the responsibility seriously.

And if you have a gift for showing kindness to others, do it gladly - **(Romans 12:4-8, NLT).**

The understanding that your purpose gives you the priviledge to make unique and valuable contributions to God's divine agenda will help you build a healthy self-identity and self-confidence. This understanding will also help you to cooperate with your team members, rather than compete with them. It will help you to stop comparing and conflicting. Instead, you will start complementing and working harmoniously with people. This will give your emotional intelligence a great boost because what you know about yourself will make you feel comfortable working with people who are different from you without feeling threatened by their abilities and accomplishments.

Paul explained this principle using the idea of the organs of our body:

Yes, there are many parts, but only one body. The eye can never say to the hand, "I don't need you." The head can't say to the feet, "I don't need you."

In fact, some parts of the body that seems weakest and least important are actually the most necessary. And the parts we regard as less honorable are those we clothe with the greatest care. So we carefully protect those parts that should not be seen, while the more honorable parts do not require this special care.

So God has put the body together such that extra honor and care are given to those parts that have less dignity - **(1 Corinthians 12:20-24, NLT)**.

When you understand and embrace the principle in this chapter, you will not fall prey to the propaganda that some human beings are "more equal" than others. You will not allow other people's opinions of you to become your fact.

Your uniqueness and originality have vested upon you inestimable value. Do not lower your value by looking down on yourself. Do not lower your value by trying to be someone else. You are created an original. If you try to be like someone else, the best you can be is a copy of that person. The fact is the original copy of an artwork is usually higher priced that any copy of that same artwork.

Your callings and gifting were decided by God before He created you. Be contented with whom He has made you to be and celebrate yourself. Take time to explore and develop your gifting rather than wishing that you have someone else's kind of gifting.

No gift or calling of God is better or greater than the other.

NO PURPOSE IS BETTER THAN THE OTHER

On the last day, God is not going to judge you on the basis of someone else's gifting or talent. He will judge you on the basis of your gifting and calling.

Anyone who boasts because of his or her gifting and belittles other people's gifts or contributions is ignorant of how God works.

There is nothing we have that has not been given to us (1 Corinthians 4:7).

You should also understand that having gifts and talents mean taking on responsibilities. That is why it is written: *"Unto whom much is given, much is expected"*- **(Luke 12:48)**.

God created you with your own special gifting. By your gifting, God has carved out a place for you in this world where you will be valued, celebrated and where you will be irreplaceable.

A person's gift makes room for him, and leads him before important people- **(Proverbs 18:16)**.

PRINCIPLE #15
PURPOSE IS THE ONLY SOURCE OF FULFILMENT

FULFILLMENT IS NOT A GOAL

The word "fulfillment" creates a big issue in our modern world. We see people do all kinds of unimaginable things in their curious search to make sense of life's meaning.

Some people think that having a lot of money will bring fulfillment and they spend the better part of their lives pursuing the acquisition of money. They achieve their goals and acquire massive amounts of wealth, only to discover that there is this deep level of un-fulfillment in their hearts that cannot be explained. Some are buried in their careers of choice, climbing the organizational ladders with the thoughts that they will find fulfillment at the top. Such people get to the top or even decide to own the ladders and then discover that the idea of a golden pot at the end of the rainbow is a fantasy.

Some people while single are busy dreaming of Mr. or Ms. Right to make them happy and satisfied in life. Several others use drugs, sex, and power as a means of finding the answer to the quest for fulfillment. The list of options people explore as pathways to happiness and fulfillment is endless and unimaginable.

A great wave of identity confusion and depression is sweeping over every nation on the earth. So many options and pathways are chosen but many have lost their sense of direction and purpose for living. At the core of most manifested depression is a sense of purposelessness, helplessness, and hopelessness.

Human wisdom says that the best way to find joy and happiness is to focus on yourself but the wisdom of God says that you find your life by giving it away.

If you cling to your life, you will lose it; but if you give up your life for me, you will find it.
-(Matthew 10:39).

Divine Purpose is the only known and sure pathway to human fulfilment. It is the ultimate cure for hopelessness and depression. Purpose unleashes a lifelong journey into inexhaustible joy, fulfilment, excitement, and discoveries.

When you are at the centre of God's purpose for your life, you can never run short of ideas of what to do and where to go. Life's possibilities are boundless and the impact is unlimited. There is no boring moment. Challenges may confront you but there is the assurance of victory and growth.

PURPOSE IS SOURCE OF FULFILMENT

1 Corinthians 2:9 says: *No eye has seen, no ear has heard, and no mind has imagined what God has prepared for those who love him.*

It is most interesting that the vision and ideas God plants in your heart are usually as unique as you are.

Deep seated inner peace and fulfilment is God's created "barometer" that helps us to determine how close or how far we are from the centre of God's purpose for our lives.

You may experience life's storms and challenges all around you but when you are at the centre of God's purpose for your life; you will have this conviction and deep-seated inner assurance that ALL shall be well.

And we KNOW that God causes EVERYTHING to work together for the good of those who love God and are called according to his PURPOSE for them. **-(Romans 8:28, NLT).**

PRINCIPLE #16
PURPOSE IS OFTEN MULTIPLE

PURPOSE UNFOLDS IN PHASES

Then God said, "Let there be lights in the firmament of the heavens to divide the day from the night; and let them be for signs and seasons, and for days and years; and let them be for lights in the firmament of the heavens to give light on the earth"; and it was so.

Then God made two great lights: the greater light to rule the day, and the lesser light to rule the night. He made the stars also.

God set them in the firmament of the heavens to give light on the earth, 18 and to rule over the day and over the night, and to divide the light from the darkness. And God saw that it was good
- (Genesis 1:14-18, NKJV).

The principal function of the sun is to give light. But there are many more functions of the sun, which include but are not limited to:

1. Rule and govern the day

2. Separate between light and darkness

3. Mark times and seasons, days, and years.

King David of the Bible is well known for confronting and defeating Goliath in battle (1 Samuel 16). But during his days, he operated in different and multiple roles. He started out at a very young age as a shepherd (1 Samuel 17:34). He was, at a point in his life, recognised as a very skilful singer and harp player (1 Samuel 16:18). He was even invited to the palace to play the harp for King Saul.

David later became a warrior-king in Judah and, a king over all of Israel. A large portion of the book of Psalms was written by David. That established him as a composer and songwriter. Another little-known role that David operated in was that of a prophet. Some of David's writings are prophetic. As a matter of fact, he prophesied in several places in the book of Psalms about the Messiah.

For example, in **Psalm 34:20**, David wrote:

He protects all his bones, not one of them will be broken.

This particular prophecy was fulfilled in the life of Jesus and recorded in the book of John:

But when they came to Jesus and found that he was already dead, they did not break his legs. These things happened so that the scripture would be fulfilled: 'Not one of his bones will be broken
- **(John 19:33, 36).**

So we can confidently say that David operated in the following roles:

1. Shepherd

2. Mistral /Singer

3. Songwriter

4. Warrior

5. King

6. Prophet

If we look at the life of Jesus, we will notice that His principal assessment and purpose was to be the *Lamb of God who takes away the sin of the world.* **-(John 1:29).**

But Jesus operated in many roles and ministered to the needs of mankind from multiple dimensions. In fact, He was "beautiful" for the entire human situation that was presented to him. He is:

1. The Bread of Life

2. The Good Shepherd

3. The Door to the Father

4. The Water of Life

5. The Light of the World

6. The Great Healer

7. And many more.

Our purpose is a mystery that is unsearchable except revealed by God. Our purpose is also unfolded in phases and as we go along our journey in life. There are things you never know you have the capacity to accomplish until God brings challenges or opportunities across your path that unravels your potential. Such experience becomes a life discovery for you.

I used to be a shy, super introvert and never believed I could ever become a public speaker and a people leader. But along my God's orchestrated journey of life, I have been blessed by covenant friends and mentors who saw what I could not see about myself. They encouraged me to step out and deploy my potential. I have been blessed with confident leaders who were never threatened to share their platforms so I could learn the ropes and find my own confidence. Such leaders are uncommon.

When you walk the pathway of purpose you will soon discover that all you are now is not all you can be; all you are doing now is just a tip of the iceberg of what God can accomplish through your life.

Your purpose, potential, and opportunities will continue to unravel as you move from one season of life to another. Some activities that are highly prioritized now might not even be on your radar screen in times to come because they have passed their season.

The possibilities of a life of purpose are unfathomable and inexhaustible.

Every season comes with its full package of assignments, provisions, opportunities, connections, challenges and discoveries.

PURPOSE IS OFTEN MULTIPLE

A life of purpose is never boring; rather, it is full of hope, anticipation, and expectation because you never know...

PRINCIPLE #17
PURPOSE IS INTERDEPENDENT

LIFE IS CREATED FOR CONNECTION

But our bodies have many parts, and God has put each part just where he wants it. How strange a body would be if it had only one part!

Yes, there are many parts, but only one body. The eye can never say to the hand, "I don't need you." The head can't say to the feet, "I don't need you
- (1 Corinthians 12:18-21, NLT).

In the above scriptures, Paul the apostle illustrated the interdependent nature of purpose in the body system: *"The eye can never say to the hand, 'I don't need you.' The head can't say to the feet, 'I don't need you.'"*

Divine purpose cannot be fulfilled in isolation. If you sever an organ from the body, the organ will shrivel and die. An organ only stays alive and makes vital contributions when it is connected to the body system.

Even though Jesus came to the earth as the beloved Son of God and Saviour of the world, He couldn't have fulfilled His purpose alone. He did not just appear on the surface of the earth but was conceived and carried in the womb for nine months by Mary.

From time to time, Mary relied on the support of Joseph, her husband, to cope with the challenges associated with conceiving and birthing the Messiah. When they needed to escape at night from Jerusalem to Egypt, it was Joseph who mobilised his wife and the boy Jesus, according to the instruction that God gave to him through an angel (Matthew 2:13-14).

When Jesus was born and in a manger, wise men from the east came and presented Him with gifts. One of their gift items was gold. That would have been an important and handy resource as the family urgently migrated from Jerusalem to Egypt and then to Nazareth.

As you walk in the path of purpose, there are people and resources that will attend to you. God orchestrates it all to help you fulfil your purpose.

And we know that God causes everything to work together for the good of those who love God and are called according to his purpose for them (Romans 8:28).

John the Baptist was sent by God ahead of Jesus Christ to prepare the way, baptize Him, and also introduce Him to Israel.

Several other people, apart from the disciples, showed up at one point or the other and added value to the life and ministry of Jesus Christ. Such people included:

1. The boy with five loaves of bread and two fishes (John 6:1-14)

2. Mary Magdalene (John 12:3)

3. The man who surrendered his colt (Matthew 21:1-8)

4. The man who provided the upper room and meal for the Last Supper (Luke 22:7-13)

5. Joseph of Arimathea who assumed responsibility for the body and burial of Jesus Christ, after crucifixion. He also gave up his own tomb to be used for the burial of Jesus
(John 19:38, John 19:39-40, Matthew 27:60).

The life and ministry of Jesus vividly painted the picture of how interdependent our purposes in life are and how purpose cannot be fulfilled in isolation. We all need the right people and the right resources to be available at the right time for our purposes to be fulfilled.

Sometimes, the people and resources will show up on their own while at other times, we need to reach out and ask for them. For example, Jesus sent His disciples to go and ask for the colt, even though it was in prophecy that He would ride on a donkey on His last visit to Jerusalem
(Zechariah 9:9, Matthew 21:5).

You need to understand and embrace this principle so that you can value and celebrate the people God has positioned around you. These are people in your life who are contributing one way or the other towards the fulfilment of your God-given purpose. The principle also shows that there are people who are waiting for your contributions and support as they pursue their purposes in life.

Lastly, we need to pay attention to how this principle plays out in nature and in the universe. We know that the earth depends on the light and warmth from the sun and moon to fulfil the purpose of sustaining human, animal, and plant lives on earth. We know how the moon depends on the light from the sun to fulfil the purpose of ruling over the night. We also know about the gaseous exchange of oxygen and carbon dioxide between man and plant, which helps to sustain humans, animals, and the plants.

The Principle is that purpose is interdependent. Purpose cannot be fulfilled in isolation.

PRINCIPLE #18
PURPOSE IS PERMANENT

The gifts and the calling of God are irrevocable (Romans 11:29).

YOUR LIFE'S CALLING IS GOD'S DIVINE PURPOSE FOR YOUR LIFE.

Your gifts are the potentials and talents you are given as resources to fulfil your divine calling.

A reference to **Principle #2:** *Purpose Precedes Creation* will shed more light on the principle in this chapter. If you understand that your purpose was decided before you were created and that you were uniquely and meticulously created to fulfil your purpose, then you will appreciate the fact that a change of purpose will require a total change of design. That is why the gifts and callings of God are irrevocable.

It is absolutely difficult, if not impossible, to change the purpose of a product after the manufacturing has been completed, especially products with inbuilt hardware.

For example, how easy is it to change a washing machine to a dishwasher? A massive reconstruction work will be required to achieve this. You cannot say that your dishwasher is broken and then you just pack all your dirty dishes into you washing machine to get them washed. Although both are for washing, they are meant for different kinds of washing.

Each product is designed with the capacity to accomplish the purpose for which it was manufactured. You cannot say that your refrigerator is broken and then place your groceries into your dishwasher for safe keeping.

Let us also imagine a plan to change your dishwasher to a refrigerator or vice versa. I think it will require less time and resources to build a refrigerator from scratch than to try and repurpose a dishwasher to a refrigerator.

That is why the gifts and the callings of God are irrevocable.

Another example is that of a car and an airplane. Both are meant for different purposes, and they are designed to accomplish those purposes. No one can fly a normal car except the car is designed and constructed with the capacity to fly. How fascinating can it be to see an airplane running on land as a bus and picking up passengers at the bus stops? What will happen to the wings as it drives on land? How will people board the plane at the bus stops?

That is what happens when we try to purpose ourselves into activities outside of our callings.

What if I decide to take an airplane into my workshop, deconstruct it and change it into a car? Does the reconstruction change the original plan and intention for which the airplane was made?

WHY MANY PEOPLE ARE NOT HAPPY

Despite the advancement in technology, increased life choices, and massive entertainment opportunities, there is an unprecedented level of unhappiness and depression in our world.

It seems that the farther we move away from the truth that there is a purposeful Creator, and we try to do our own things in our own ways, the more we plunge the human family into the abyss of confusion, conflicts, fear, and hopelessness.

Some people have spent all their lives trying to be or do what they are not created for. They do the job they hate for the boss they cannot tolerate. People live their lives majoring in the minors and minoring in the majors. We have our values and priority systems turned upside down. How convenient is it to walk when you wear the right shoe on the left leg and vice versa? That is what happens in life when we do not accomplish our purposes and misplace our priorities.

You enjoy peace of mind and serendipity when you are doing what you were created to do.

Enough is enough with chasing after lies, shadows or mirage. It is time to get real with your life. You need to move on from just existing to living to fulfil the purpose for which you were born.

TAMPERING WITH NATURE

The entire universe was meticulously created by the wisdom of God and held in delicate balance. As human beings, we sometimes assume roles that are far bigger than us, especially when it comes to tampering with nature and creation.

When we look at our world, we see a lot of damaging changes to the environment, destabilised ecological systems and unusual changes in the weather system. Most of these are because we keep tampering with the original plans of God for our world. Where purpose is not known, abuse is inevitable.

The introduction of all kinds of growth hormones into our food (vegetable, beef, chicken, etc.) is unleashing all kinds of health issue that mankind has never known or experienced before.

As human beings, our knowledge about ourselves and our world is still very limited, despite the 21st-century breakthroughs in science and technology. When we tamper with the delicate balance in our world or in our bodies, we may activate certain ripple effects that we are least prepared to handle or curtail.

That is why it is disturbing to see how we tinker with our minds and bodies using surgeries and medication without considering the long-term consequences of our physical, mental, and emotional stability.

I will conclude this chapter by reminding you that your life is not a product of random chance but rather, a product of a loving, meticulous, and purposeful God.

Before I made you in your mother's womb, I knew you. Before you were born, I chose you for a special work - **(Jeremiah 1:5, ERV).**

PRINCIPLE #19
PURPOSE IS PRESERVATIVE

For everything there is an appointed time, and an appropriate time for every activity on earth (Ecclesiastes 3:1, NET Bible).

YOUR DAYS ARE NUMBERED.

To everything there is a season, A TIME for every PURPOSE under heaven. - (Ecclesiastes 3:1).

So far, we have covered some fundamental principles of purpose that are foundational to the present principle:

Principle #1 - There is a Purposeful Creator

Principle #2 - Purpose Precedes Creation

Principle #7 - Every Purpose Has Its Time and Season

There is a time and a season allotted to every purpose. God makes everything beautiful (appropriate) in its time (Ecclesiastes 3:11).

It is on the basis of Principle #7 - Every Purpose Has Its Time and Season that Jesus said:

We must quickly carry out the tasks assigned us by the one who sent us. The night is coming, and then no one can work - **(John 9:4, NLT)**.

Daytime is the time of your life. It is the time allotted to you by God to fulfil your purpose. Your night time is the time of sleep - the sleep of death.

Several verses in the Bible refer to death as sleep and I will give you three of them:

After he had said this, he (Jesus) went on to tell them, "Our friend Lazarus has fallen asleep; but I am going there to wake him up" - **(John 11:11)**.

Listen, I tell you a mystery: We will not all sleep, but we will all be changed - **(1 Corinthian 15:51)**.

For if we believe that Jesus died and rose again, so also we believe that God will bring with him those who have fallen asleep as Christians
- **(1 Thessalonians 4:14)**.

You may need to read the context of the Bible passages to get a clear picture of the meaning of those statements. However, our focus is on death being referred to as sleep in those scriptures.

At the night time of life, the opportunity to fulfill purpose ceases. The following scriptures attest to this fact:

I will not die; instead, I will live to tell what the LORD has done - **(Psalm 118:17)**.

The dead cannot sing praises to the LORD, for they have gone into the silence of the grave.
- **(Psalm 115:17)**.

PURPOSE IS PRESERVATIVE

For the dead cannot praise you; they cannot raise their voices in praise. Those who go down to the grave can no longer hope in your faithfulness. - (Isaiah 38:18).

No matter how full of life you might feel right now, there is a designated period called the "night time." It is the time when no one can work because all life activities cease during this period.

I Will Give You Full A Lifespan.

In **Exodus 23:26**, God says: The number of your days I will fulfil. The New International Version of the same verse says: *"I will give you a full lifespan."*

Related to this scripture is the prayer of David in **Psalm 102:24** where he prayed to God: "*Do not take me away in the midst of my days.*"

So we can say that there is a beginning of life; there is a mid-life and there is an end of life. The FULL lifespan is the life allotted for the completion of the assignment of life.

Your purpose is the reason you were born in the first place. And because the dead cannot fulfil purpose, your purpose preserves you so you can have a full lifespan and the chance to fulfill your assignment.

Despite every attempt on the life of Jesus Christ, His purpose kept Him alive until the assignment was fully completed.

Jesus knew that his mission was now finished, and to fulfil Scripture he said, "I am thirsty"

When he had received the drink, Jesus said, "It is finished." With that, he bowed his head and gave up his spirit - **(John 19:28, 30).**

Paul, the apostle also had similar experiences. He was involved in a lot of challenging life situations. He was beaten; he was imprisoned on several occasions; he was involved in a ship wreck; he was bitten by a highly venomous snake; arrangements were made to assassinate him but purpose kept him alive.

In *2 Timothy 4:6-8(NIV)* apostle Paul says:

For I am already being poured out like a drink offering, and the time for my departure is near.

I have fought the good fight, I have FINISHED the race, I have kept the faith.

Now there is in store for me the crown of righteousness, which the Lord, the righteous Judge, will award to me on that day—and not only to me, but also to all who have longed for his appearing.

When we look at these two great characters in the Bible (Jesus and Paul), we notice how the word "FINISHED" was part of their "valedictory speeches." Both of them seem to place strong emphasis, not just on doing but FINISHING their callings and assignments.

Then Jesus explained: "*My nourishment comes from doing the will of God, who sent me, and from finishing his work -* **(John 4:34).**

No situation was powerful enough to take their lives until their works were completed. This is because Purpose is a Preservative.

God created you for a purpose. He gave you your lifespan so you can fulfil that purpose. Your lifespan is set, and it is an adequate measure for you to complete your calling. The decision to wisely use those times to focus on the right thing is up to you.

You have decided the length of our lives. You know how many months we will live, and we are not given a minute longer - **(Job 14:5, NLT)**.

Your eyes saw my unformed body; all the days ordained for me were written in your book before one of them came to be (Psalm 139:16, NIV).

God preserves your life so you can fulfil the purpose He has given to you. That is why you should make your life count. You need to discover your calling and passionately commit to fulfilling it.

At this point, let us put everything into the right perspective:

1. You are not a creature of chance; you are a creation of a purposeful God.

2. You have a calling to fulfill and a purpose to complete. That is the reason you were created. That is the reason you were born.

3. You have an allotted time or lifespan to accomplish the purpose.

4. Until this allotted time is completed, God preserves your life.

What should be your desire and prayer? It should be like the pray of Jesus:

"Dear Father God, my desire and commitment are to do and complete the assignment that you have given me here on Earth."

Do not forget that you do not have all the time in the world, and you need to be laser- focused on the task ahead.

Paul said: *Brothers and sisters, I do not consider myself to have attained this. Instead I am single-minded: Forgetting the things that are behind and reaching out for the things that are ahead, with this goal in mind, I strive toward the prize of the upward call of God in Christ Jesus -* **(Philippians3:12-14).**

A prize await those who fulfil their callings but there is the need to be laser- focused, to reach out and to strive towards fulfilling that calling of God on your life. As long as there is breath in your nostrils, you can keep taking giant strides for Jesus.

PRINCIPLE #20
PURPOSE DETERMINES DEMAND

Healthy people don't need a doctor--sick people do. I have come to call not those who think that they are righteous, but those who know they are sinners - (Mark 2:17).

YOU ARE A PROBLEM SOLVER

Your purpose will determine those who will demand and seek out the solution that you have been created to provide.

Everyone God has created is a problem solver. A lawyer solves legal problems; a doctor solves medical problems, and a dentist solves teeth problems. But no one can be a one-size- fits-all kind of a person. You have specific gifting and you have specific audiences.

Products also solve problems. That is even the basis of business and productions. Business is about providing and delivering goods and services that will solve human problems, at a profit. Different kinds of products or services will appeal to different customers.

That is why we have such massive amounts of product types, ranges, and methods of delivery. That is why we have different styles of music, clothing, cars, phones, radio and TV stations, hotels, and restaurants. We live in a generation of information and options overload. A person's perceived problems will determine the solutions they seek out.

God has created you as a solution to some people's problem. You are not just here on earth to add to the population. No matter the circumstances surrounding your conception and your birth, your birth was not an accident.

No matter how you feel about your life at the moment, I want you to know that you are a creature of great value. God has gifted so much into you that you cannot afford to let your potential become redundant. People and generations are waiting for the solution only you can provide.

Maybe you have even experienced rejection and failure before and you are so afraid to take another plunge. I want you to know you are not sent to everyone. Everyone will not accept or celebrate you, your gifting and the solution you have been equipped to provide. So, go to where you are celebrated, not where you are tolerated.

Paul, the Apostle - A Case Study

One person whose life clearly demonstrates this principle in this passage was Paul, the apostle. Just after his spectacular conversion experience on the way to Damascus, where he was going to arrest followers of Christ, God sent a believer named Ananias to pray for him. God told Ananias:

This man is my CHOSEN INSTRUMENT to proclaim my name to the GENTILES and their kings and to the people of Israel - **(Acts 9:15, NIV).**

Paul's life before his conversion shows how far we can move away from the centre of God's plan for our lives. God created and chose Paul to advance His work but he was actively opposing the work he was created to advance.

Paul's purpose and calling were not determined at the time of his conversion. Rather they were established before he was born.

Principle #2 says, "Purpose Precedes Creation."

God told Jeremiah:

BEFORE I formed you in the womb, I KNEW ALL ABOUT YOU. - **(Jeremiah 1:5).**

In **Psalm 139:16** David said, *Your eyes saw my unformed body and ALL the days you appointed for me were written in your books BEFORE I was born.*

According to the revelation in Hebrews 10:9, when Jesus came into the world, He prayed to the Father God: *"I have come to do your will according to what is written about me in your books."*

I decided to make reference to this scripture just as a reminder of the TRUTH that was established in **Principle #2** that *"Purpose Precedes Creation"* and to make the point, as said earlier, that Paul's purpose and calling were not determined at his conversion.

Paul himself, after his conversion, professed that God chose him before he was born.

You know what I was like when I followed the Jewish religion--how I violently persecuted God's church. I did my best to destroy it. I was far ahead of my fellow Jews in my zeal for the traditions of my ancestors. But even before I was born, God chose me and called me by his marvellous grace.
- (Galatians 1:13 –15).

Paul went on to become one of the most outstanding apostles. This can be attributed to the fact that he was fully aware of God's calling and assignment for his life. He got the divine revelation of whom God created him to be and what God created him to do. This is in line with Principle #4: Purpose Is Discovered by Revelation. Purpose is not discovered by human opinion about you. That was why Paul said:

But when God, who set me apart from my mother's womb and called me by his grace, was pleased to reveal his Son in me so that I might preach him among the GENTILES, my immediate response was not to consult any human being
- **(Galatians 1:15-16).**

There are a lot of people who have abandoned their God-given purposes and assignments because they are following human opinions.

In **Principle #4:** *Purpose Is Discovered by Revelation*, we saw how the family of Zacharias wanted to name his son Zacharias Junior after the name of his father. This was a great idea but not God's idea. The child, John the Baptist, was conceived by revelation. He was also named John by divine revelation. But many times, human opinions conflict with divine revelation. That is why many people have missed their callings and are unhappily locked into jobs and career that are inconsistent with their life callings and gifting.

When it comes to the matter of purpose and your life calling, you cannot but get it right. Plus, your source of information must be reliable. That is not to say that you cannot make consultation with wise, mature, and spiritual leaders with track records. But the fact still remains that ultimately, you will be answerable to God, not to man.

Paul was so confident about his life calling that he declared it wherever he had the opportunity. For example:

In view of the fact that I am an apostle to the GENTILES, I magnify my ministry
- **(Romans 11:13, HSBC).**

Though I am the least deserving of all God's people, he graciously gave me the privilege of telling the GENTILES about the endless treasures available to them in Christ - **(Ephesians 3:8, NLT).**

For the same God who worked through Peter as the apostle to the Jews also worked through me as the apostle to the GENTILES - **(Galatians 2:8, NLT).**

Your purpose and your assignment are to a specific group of people; in our modern day lingo, we call them your "TRIBE." Those are the people who will most likely respond to you. For example, your calling might be to children, teens, young adults, singles, the divorced, single mums, couples, people in mid-life, older adults, people in crises, people in need of recovery from drugs or alcohol, people going through health challenges. The list is inexhaustible.

The dimension of your assignment may be focused on meeting the physical, mental, emotional or spiritual needs of your "TRIBE." For example, a number of people might be sent to teenagers but one might be sent to meet their mental needs through education and the other might meet their emotional needs through counseling. Another person might be sent to meet their physical and identity needs through clothing and fashion. Someone else might be sent to meet their spiritual needs through a youth ministry.

The people you are sent to are also the people you are equipped and gifted to reach. Your unique personality, potential, and passion were specially designed so you can minister to the needs of your "TRIBE." Your God-given personality, potential, and passion are resources that you can tap into to fulfill your purpose.

Paul had an unprecedented revelation from God about the eternal agenda of God for mankind through the nation of Israel. As an apostle to the GENTILES, he was granted revelation of the big picture plan of God and how the Gentiles were made to be partakers of the Commonwealth of Israel. He had a deeper understanding of God's plan for the Gentiles than any of the apostles.

As you wait before God and allow Him to open His eternal plan for your life, you will discover that you have unprecedented wisdom and ability in your area of calling. This makes you unique and you will become a sought-after solution provider in that "niche." You will also experience outstanding levels of success and fulfillment because you are engaged in doing what you are created to do.

Unless a grain of wheat falls to the ground and dies, it remains by itself. But if it dies, it produces a large crop - **(John 12:24, HCSB).**

A very popular quote by **Zig Ziglar** says: *"You can have everything in life you want, if you will just help other people get what they want."*

PRINCIPLE #21
PURPOSE DETERMINES REWARD IN THE LIFE TO COME

People are destined to die once, and after that to face judgment - (Hebrews 9:27, NIV).

And I saw the dead, great and small, standing before the throne, and books were opened. Another book was opened, which is the book of life. The dead were judged according to what they had done as recorded in the books.

The sea gave up the dead that were in it, and death and Hades gave up the dead that were in them, and each person was judged according to what they had done.

Anyone whose name was not found written in the book of life was thrown into the lake of fire.
- *(Revelation 20:12-13, 15).*

THIS LIFE IS A PREPARATION FOR ETERNITY

In the first chapter of this book, I stated that there is time and there is eternity. Time is a chunk of timeline carved out by eternity. Time has a beginning and an end point. Eternity has no beginning or end point. Eternity existed before time began and will continue after time is no more.

This is a mystery that cannot be fathomed by our limited human minds. It is a revelation that can only be believed. It is just like the mystery of the existence of God. You cannot comprehend it with the human mind but you have the capacity in your heart to believe it because *"with the heart, man believes"* - **(Romans 10:10).** Faith cannot happen in the mind. It can only happen in the heart, which is in your spirit. That is why it is written that the *"Spirit of God bears witness with our (human) spirit that we are children of God"* - **(Romans 8:16).**

That you are a child of God cannot be fathomed with the human mind. It is just like trying to explain the internet to an ant.

In the scripture, time is also referred to as this world and eternity as the world to come (Luke 18:30). This life is the prequalification for rewards that are received in the world to come.

Revelation 20:12-13 and 15 gives a vivid picture of the judgment of all mankind at the end of this world. To have a broader perspective of the scripture, we need to look at another scripture in the New Testament:

For no one can lay any foundation other than the one we already have—Jesus Christ. Anyone who builds on that foundation may use a variety of materials—gold, silver, jewels, wood, hay, or straw.

PURPOSE DETERMINES REWARD....

But on the JUDGMENT DAY, fire will reveal what kind of work each builder has done. The fire will show if a person's WORK has any value.
- 1 Corinthians 3:11-14, (NLT).

If the WORK survives, the builder will RECEIVE A REWARD.

The two scripture verses above give us in-depth information about how life on earth will be rewarded after this life.

Revelation 20 speaks of the dead, both great and small. This is a reference to a time when all human beings will have to give the *ultimate account* of their lives here on earth.

This passage speaks of two types of books in heaven. One is simply called *"books"*- (I saw books were opened) with emphasis on the plurality of the book. This suggests multiple numbers of books. There is also another book that was opened called, "the book of life." - (ANOTHER BOOK was opened which is the Book of Life)

Looking closely at the passage, we can note that the two types of books contain two different types of information. The book of life only contains NAMES, while the other books contain WORKS that were done here on earth.

It can also be noted that there are two levels of judgments defined in that passage: The judgment of destinations — heaven or hell and the judgment of rewards.

The decision about a person's final destination after this life is determined by whether or not his or her name is in the *book of life*. The decision of how people will be rewarded is determined by what is written in the books. If a person's name is not found in the book of life, then his/her final destination is the "lake of fire" or hell. If a person's name is found in the book of life, then his/her final destination is heaven. This is the first judgment after this life. This is the judgment that determines the eternal destination of a person. Every human being who has ever lived will participate in first judgment.

Whoever scales through this first hurdle are the only people who will have the privilege of participating in the second judgment which is the judgment of rewards.

For God so loved the world that He gave His only begotten Son, that whoever believes in Him should not perish but have everlasting life
- **(John 3:16, NKJV).**

I mean that you have been saved by grace because you believed. You did not save yourselves; it was a gift from God. You are not saved by the things you have done, so there is nothing to boast about.
-**(Ephesians 2:8-9, ERV).**

Salvation is not the result of the things you have done. Salvation is a free gift from God to anyone who believes in Jesus Christ and accepted Him as Lord and Saviour, while here on earth. That simple decision will have an eternal consequence after the life on earth.

2 Corinthians 11:3 says that a lot of people will miss out on the opportunity of getting saved because of how simple and illogical the requirement is.

Romans 10:9-10 (NIV) shows us the requirement:

If you declare with your mouth, "Jesus is Lord," and believe in your heart that God raised him from the dead, you will be saved.

For it is with your heart that you believe and are justified, and it is with your mouth that you profess your faith and are saved.

In **Romans 1:16,** KJV Paul says:

For I am not ashamed of the gospel of Christ: for it is the POWER OF GOD UNTO SALVATION to EVERYONE THAT BELIEVETH; to the Jew first, and also to the Greek.

Many people expect the process of salvation to be a complicated process but it is a simple one. The difficult and complicated end of the process has been completed for us by Jesus Christ. That is why salvation is the gift of God to us through Christ Jesus.

When a person receives Jesus Christ as Lord and Saviour, he/she is saved and the person's name is written in the book of life.

Obviously, anyone whose name is not in the book of life will not be required to participate in the second stage of the judgment, which is meant to reward people for their works of advancing the kingdom of God while on the earth. The first judgment is meant to answer the question: "*What did you do with my Son Jesus? Did you accept Him or did you reject Him?*"

The second judgment is meant to answer the question: *"What did you do with the purpose and gifting that I gave to you? Did you use the time and gifting to accomplish your purpose or did you waste all the resources that were invested in you?"*

1 Corinthians 3:11-14 threw more light on the second level of judgment. This judgment is also going to produce two categories of people: those that will get rewarded for their works and those that are without any rewards.

According to the scriptures, people in both categories (those with will receive rewards and those that will have no rewards) will make heaven, but those without rewards will make heaven like someone escaping through fire.

I have fought the good fight, I have finished the race, and I have remained faithful.

*And now the prize awaits me—the crown of righteousness, which the Lord, the righteous Judge, will give me on the day of his return. And the prize is not just for me but for all who eagerly look forward to his appearing - **(2 Timothy 4:7-8, NLT).***

Paul said, "I have finished the race." There is a race to be finished. There is an assignment to be completed. It is the completion of this assignment that guarantees a full reward.

PURPOSE DETERMINES REWARD....

Your life's calling is the reason you were born and it is the race to be completed.

In **Psalm 139:16 (NIV)**, David said:

Your eyes saw my unformed body; all the days ordained for me were written in your book before one of them came to be.

Before God formed you in the womb, He knew all about you, and He saw your unformed body. He also wrote down your purpose and your assignment in His book, even before you were born.

God sent you into this world to fulfill a purpose and He is writing in His books the works that you are doing with your life on earth. It is only the works that correspond with the assignment He has given you that will be rewarded.

1 Corinthians 3 says that everything you do here on earth will be TESTED by the fire of God's judgment. Any deed that does not correspond to God's assigned purpose is classified as worthless and it is consumed by fire. Such works will go unrewarded even though the person who did the works will be saved.

That is why Christ said as He came into the world,

I have come to DO YOUR WILL, to lay down my life, ACCORDING to what is written about me in your books. - **(Hebrews 10:7).**

From the beginning, Jesus Christ was committed to fulfilling what was written about Him ahead of time in the volumes of books.

If you compare Psalm 139:19, Hebrews 10:6, and Revelation 20:12-13, we will notice that the "your book," "books" that were opened and "the volumes of books" are all and the same thing.

In Psalm 139:16 and Hebrews 10, we discover that what we are here to do were already written in the books of God even before we were born. Our assignment is to come to the earth and fulfil what has been written concerning us.

Revelation 20 gives us additional information about the books that as we live our lives on earth, our deeds are also written in the books. This goes on to say that at the beginning of your life, the volume of God's book contains the assignment you have been given and at the end of your life, it contains both the assignment you have been given and your works while you were on the earth.

So the judgment of rewards will be based on comparing the two sides of the life accounting book. This book has two sides: the "what to do" side and the "what was done" side.

To God, obedience is more important than sacrifice - **(1 Samuel 15:22).**

That is why God is not going to reward all the works done, but only works done according to purpose.

Let us imagine a scenario where Jesus Christ decided to be a physical king who fought and won freedom for the Jews from their Roman oppressors. This might go down as a great effort in the books of human history but might be worthless in the books of God. Jesus might have met the expectation of the Jews for a physical Messiah who was going to fight their battles but He would have missed the assignment of God for His life.

When Jesus saw that they were ready to force him to be their king, he slipped away into the hills by himself. -(John 6:15).

Jesus answered, "My Kingdom is not an earthly kingdom. If it were, my followers would fight to keep me from being handed over to the Jewish leaders. But my Kingdom is not of this world"- (John 18:36).

Jesus knew the assignment the Father gave Him and He refused to be distracted by any great earthly offers.

When they came to arrest Jesus Christ, Peter tried to fight back and prevent Jesus' arrest. But **John 18:11** says: *Jesus commanded Peter, "Put your sword away! Shall I not drink the cup the Father has given me?"*

If we look further at the experience of Jesus in the garden of Gethsemane, we will notice that going to the cross was not what His flesh wanted to do. He even prayed, *"If it is possible, let this cup pass over Me"*- (Matthew 26:39).

What the prayer suggests is that if it was possible God could have allowed Him not to go to the cross. Jesus going to the cross to die for the sins of mankind was the ultimate reason He was born.

John the Baptist even testified: *"Behold the lamb of God who took away the sins of the world"* - **(John 1:29).**

At the Last Supper with His disciples, Jesus gave the bread as His body that is broken and the wine as His blood that is poured out.

Jesus ended His prayer in the garden of Gethsemane with a prayer of ultimate submission to the will of the Father, *"Not My will but your will be done."*

Jesus was, *"Obedient unto death even death on the cross THEREFORE the Lord has highly exalted him and gave him a name above ALL name"* - **(Philippians 2:8).**

In our daily walk, we also experience the battle of wills. God works in us by His Spirit creating in us a desire to do His will (Philippians 2:13) but the flesh always tries to resist the will of God for our lives. Sometimes, the Devil orchestrates what looks like opportunities or open doors just to distract us from fulfilling God's purpose for our lives.

You need to know that every opportunity is not your opportunity. You need to develop the discipline to stay focused on your calling, no matter how "lucrative" the distracting offer looks.

A vivid example of the power of the big "NO" is set out in **Judges 9:8-13(HCSB)**:

The trees set out to anoint a king over themselves. They said to the olive tree, "Reign over us." But the olive tree said to them, "Should I stop giving my oil that honours both God and man, and rule over the trees?"

Then the trees said to the fig tree, "Come and reign over us." But the fig tree said to them, "Should I stop giving my sweetness and my good fruit, and rule over trees?"

Later, the trees said to the grapevine, "Come and reign over us." But the grapevine said to them, "Should I stop giving my wine that cheers both God and man, and rule over trees?"

Finally, all the trees said to the bramble, "Come and reign over us." The bramble said to the trees,

"If you really are anointing me as king over you, come and find refuge in my shade. But if not, may fire come out from the bramble and consume the cedars of Lebanon."

What are the lessons from the above story?

1. You need to know your calling and stay in your calling.

2. Every opportunity is not your opportunity.

3. You need to avoid the temptation to abandon your calling and chase after what you are not called to do.

4. Success in life is not about titles and positions but about fulfilling your calling.

5. You need to understand your area of strength and the contribution you have been created to make to mankind.

6. You need to understand the value your contribution adds to mankind.

7. If you do not understand the value you have been created to add, you will not have the discipline to say "NO."

8. People with domineering leadership styles are insecure leaders with identity crises.

My question for you as I conclude this great book is:

Are you pursuing your life calling?

DOWNLOAD THE TOOLBOX FREE

Just to say thanks for buying my book,
I would like to give you the
Ultimate Self Discovery Toolbox 100% FREE!

TO DOWNLOAD GO TO:

http://femioyewopo.com/21ipop_toolbox

Thank you

Thank You For Reading My Book!

I really appreciate all of your feedback, and
I love hearing what you have to say.

I need your input to make the next version of this book and my future books better.

Please leave me a helpful review on Amazon letting me know what you thought of the book.

Thanks so much!!
~ Femi Oyewopo

Practical Life Story

Do you have a real life story that is a proof of one or more principles in this book?

Will you like so share your story with me?

Kindly send your story to:
femi@femioyewopo.com

"We are all pencils in the hand of God."
~Mother Teresa

END NOTE

www.ingramcontent.com/pod-product-compliance
Lightning Source LLC
Chambersburg PA
CBHW032040290426
44110CB00012B/886